SUPERWOMAN

Sue

Time to let go of the cape !.

SUPERWOMAN

- HER SELL BY DATE HAS EXPIRED!

TIME TO SHOW LITTLE MISS PERFECT THE DOOR

by

Jane Kenyon

First published in Great Britain by Practical Inspiration Publishing, 2014
© Jane Kenyon 2014
Cover and illustrations by Emily Harvey
www.eharvey.co.uk

ISBN (print): 978-1-910056-20-2
ISBN (ebook): 978-1-910056-21-9

dedication

To all the women who have stepped up and become Well Heeled Divas since we launched in 2007. You have inspired me in so many ways and opened the door to my legacy. You rock!

contents

acknowledgements

I would like to take this opportunity to thank the hundreds of women past and present who have contributed to my awareness and action on this journey over the past 20 years, from the first depiction of Superwoman by Shirley Conran in 1978 to the latest writing on embracing our vulnerability by Brene Brown in 2010.

The following women and their work have had a profound influence on my passion and life purpose: Oprah, Marianne Williamson, Germaine Greer, Caitlin Moran, Natasha Walter, Louise L. Hay and Eve Ensler.

I honour all the women who have stepped up with courage and confidence to 'have it all' on their own terms and I continue to be inspired by all the female pioneers making it possible for our daughters to truly believe they can be, do and have anything they so desire, on their terms, in their female energy, NOW!

Thanks also to Alison Jones, Emily Harvey, Louise Wood, Holly Kenyon and my number one fan, Tony Davies.

And finally I salute all the superwomen brave enough to dump the cape and the badge for a more authentic life.

preface

As I begin this book I would like to pay tribute to all the other women who have written about superwoman over the years. She is not a new phenomenon, but she is definitely past her sell by date and ready for extinction. She may have been needed and the perfect model in the 70s and 80s but today she is old school, tired, over-reliant on male energy and not fit for purpose.

However, I also know she will not disappear in a puff of smoke just because you say 'superwoman must die' three times whilst clicking your red stilettos together and closing your eyes! We have come to see the Little Miss Perfect cape as a badge of honour in the battle for so-called equality, for having it all. It's been our armour in the fight against sexism and media exploitation. Letting her go demands courage and a leap of faith.

I get it and I understand the fear in letting her go, but let her go we must: she is sabotaging our right to be real, to be authentic, to be us. Aiming to be perfect at everything has become our drug of choice and it is destroying our authenticity and messing with our mojo!

Ripping off the Miss Invincible badge will take time and gumption but I know in doing so we will be empowered all over again, only this time the outcome will be sustainable because we will be presenting our authenticity to the world, as opposed to attempting to live up to someone else's fake ideal.

All I ask is that you keep your heart and mind open as you come with me on a journey to say farewell to superwoman and the illusion of perfectionism, and recognise along the way you are already enough.

introduction

I know I am supposed to outline my reasons for writing this book here, but where to start?

How about this…

In conversation with my 28-year-old, high-flying bank relationship manager: 'It's unusual for me to get on with someone like you Jane, you know, a feminist. But you are not like those other feminists are you?'

What other feminists, I wondered.

'You know, those women that hate men.'

My response was my classic: 'Correct Karen, I love men, I just don't want to be one and nor do I expect to be subservient to one.'

As I left and reflected on the exchange, at first I giggled then I was hit by a sense of sadness. All our pioneering, such progress, such sacrifices made in order for her to even have the opportunities she now has in a high street bank, and in the 21st century she still thinks we are all bra-burning, tub-thumping men haters (another name I have been called too). This was a humbling moment.

Or how about this…

In conversation with a 15-year-old girl who was excitedly telling me about her date with a 38-year-old man she had just met on Facebook: 'Ahhh, Jane, he is so cool and looks after me so well, he has even agreed to pay for my boob job when I am 18.'

The statement that her boob job was somehow an entitlement upset me beyond measure even before I had time to digest the Facebook courtship or the age concern! Fortunately, I was in a mentoring relationship with this young girl at the time so I had many opportunities to help her reframe those views and build her self-esteem.

Or how about this…

A homemade banner I spotted on a roundabout on my way to a meeting in the seaside town of Blackpool: 'Happy 30th Birthday Gran.'

Or how about this…

In conversation with a successful female entrepreneur, divorced with 2 kids: 'Well, Jane, I do not need a man and to be honest I do not think it is fair to bring another man into my life until the children are at university and have left home.'

'OK, so how old are your children?'

'Josh is 4 and Olivia is 5.'

I took a deep breath. 'So am I to accept that you are not allowed to have a relationship or be loved for at least the next 14 years???? What kind of a life model is that to pass on?'

Or how about this…

In conversation with a twenty-something female lawyer in a big firm in the UK on the subject of career advancement and children: 'I think it is fair and reasonable that women should choose children or career, you cannot expect men to take you seriously if you want children as it always puts your career and their business second, and women with kids are so unreliable.'

Oh boy, where to start…

I know and believe there has never been a better time to be a woman. We are at the peak of our emotional development, we have more opportunities and choices open to us than ever before. The corporate world needs us more than ever, the feminisation of leadership is coming, entrepreneurship is becoming a serious option for many and if you believe all the projections, by 2020 women will control over 65% of all the personal wealth in this country.

But I feel as though we are losing the plot, we are not looking or listening. We are permanently exhausted from playing the superwoman game, we are buying into the media/commercial hype about the need to look younger and thinner, we are staying small and insignificant at work and in business for fear of being seen as too aggressive or male. Some of us have made a switch and accepted that to get on and up we have to behave like men, and we are now finding out that this does not work in our personal life. We are straitjacketed by the need to be perfect at everything – the best lover, the best domestic goddess, the best boss, the best wife, the best Mum at the school gate, the best neighbour, the best daughter, the best best friend – this is a master class in self-flagellation and we excel here too!

In essence we have fallen out of love with ourselves. We no longer seem to value the very things that make us female – emotions, intuition, passion, vulnerability. We focus our attention on others and what they expect from us, people-pleasing to excess, and then wonder why we are exhausted, confused and lost.

I have worked with hundreds, if not thousands of women over the past 10 years as a coach, trainer, speaker and mentor and no-one is more passionate about female empowerment than me, however, it is time to reflect and ask ourselves some serious questions: Can we have it all? What messages are we passing on to our children via our life choices? What does an acceptable work/life balance look like? Do we want househusbands? How does our obsession with looking good impact on our daughters' self-esteem and body image? Is it OK to give birth at 16 or 65? Should we sacrifice our values and identity at work? Is it OK to show vulnerability sometimes?

This book represents my musings, my opinions and my views on the challenges facing 21st-century women. My conclusions are my own, but have been influenced by all the courageous women I have worked with over the years and who have invested in this book by sharing their stories – they know who they are and I salute them. It is not an academic thesis, it is an observation and a plea from the heart from me to you to think about the messages we are sending out to our daughters, our sons and our men. It is a call for action for us to embrace sisterhood again, unite in our common cause, love one another, and celebrate our feminine souls. It is food for thought on our journey so far. Are we getting it vaguely right, or have we lost our identity in our pursuit of equality and the eternal search for a work/life balance?

This book is all about YOU. So put the kettle on, put your feet up and give yourself a gift – the gift of reflection, refocus and possibly redirection as I invite you to open your heart and embrace your authentic, feminine self. She is waiting to be acknowledged and recognised. She is fed up of being ignored!

I cannot put this any better than Marianne Williamson and I am not even going to try:

'Our deepest fear is not that we are inadequate. Our deepest fear is that we are powerful beyond measure. It is our light, not our darkness that most frightens us. We ask ourselves, Who am I to be brilliant, gorgeous, talented, fabulous? Actually, who are you not to be? You are a child of God. Your playing small does not serve the world. There's nothing enlightening about shrinking so that other people won't feel insecure around you. We are all meant to shine, as children do. We were born to make manifest the glory of God that is within us. It's not just in some of us; it's in everyone. And as we let our own light shine, we unconsciously give other people permission to do the same. As we are liberated from our own fear, our presence automatically liberates others.'

A Return to Love, Marianne Williamson

My wish for you all is that you recognise what you need to do to shine. People that shine are very easy to spot, they stand out a mile, they literally sparkle. Be one of them. Life is too short to watch other people shine.

Love and light,

Jane

Can we have it all? The question on everyone's lips, but to be honest, I don't remember asking for IT ALL and I am not really sure what IT ALL is. Are you? From what I can gather, having it all means doing everything we have always done but now having a job too!

I feel like we are being punished for suggesting we are as capable as men in the workplace or even thinking that equality could work. Whenever I hear the words 'having it all' I feel like I am getting a dressing-down from some old Dickensian headmaster: 'See, dear, you wanted it all and now you have it: not all it's cracked up to be, is it dear? Well now what are you going to do?

May I suggest you get back in the kitchen with renewed vigour and all will be forgiven!'

But I have to object. We do NOT have equality. It is an illusion, one a certain variety of men love to throw at us like a weapon with their 'told you so' accusations. But they are wrong. The playing field is absolutely NOT level at the most fundamental level. We have no political power; only 1 in 5 MPs are female. We have no economic parity, as the pay gap continues to widen. We occupy too few places at the top of corporate tree; only 17% of senior jobs are held by women[1]. And we certainly do not have freedom from violence, with domestic abuse on the increase and the conviction rate in rape cases standing at a mere 6%, with up to 95% of rapes not even reported[2]! Men and women are categorically NOT equal in society and this cannot be ignored in the debate.

If the IT ALL everyone is referring to is simply a professional life and children, then what's the big deal? This would be doable, but I fear this is not really the question, is it?

Here are some recent headlines from the UK press:

> *The Work-Wife Balance – Not even Madonna can have it all at home and work so should women give up the fight for power?*

---

[1] Catalyst report *The Bottom Line: Connecting Corporate Performance & Gender Diversity*, 2004
[2] UK Crime Statistics, 2012

High-earning women less likely to read at bedtime

End of the hourglass – Career women usher in straighter female form

High heels at work – the debate begins...

Make-up & high heels at 7 – It's time we mothers stopped our girls becoming mini sex objects

Flexible working likely to backfire on women

Career, marriage, children... depression – Is it payback time for the have-it-all generation?

If you read past the headline, regardless of the topic, women always appear to be the problem – when literacy rates amongst young children are falling it's our fault for going out to work, because we dare to wear high heels to work Health & Safety and the Trade Unions are up in arms, career women are portrayed as women baying for power. When we hold down jobs we are somehow changing the shape of the female form. Early sexual-isation of **all** young girls is our fault. And the classic – depression is payback. The last headline referring to depression is lifted from the front cover of Britain's multi-award-winning YOU magazine. With 4.1 million readers, YOU is the top-performing magazine in the Sunday supplement marketplace. On the same front cover the other two headlines were 'THE MAKE-UP MIRACLE WORKERS – Introducing the mascaras that make your lashes grow' and 'LET'S DO LUST – Put the passion back on the marital menu'. See any patterns here?

It's easy to say this is just the press and no one takes any notice, but how accurate is that? Are we not absorbing some of this stuff subconsciously? If we are not affected by it at all how come the cosmetic surgery industry is booming and we are all on permanent diets? Do we get the media we deserve? Are they simply reflecting the values of our society? Or are they actively directing it? This is a question for you. Personally, I refuse to be a victim of the media and always read between the lines, if I read at all! But I wonder how typical I am here? Subconsciously, are we absorbing these messages and beating ourselves up? There is no denying that the media has a huge impact on our values and beliefs.

the glossies – making us feel good, right?

Pick up any glossy magazine on any day of the week and by the time you have turned the last page you can be forgiven for feeling a little inadequate. The airbrushed images and messages simply support our unrealistic goals of perfection. The messages are powerful and subliminal. If you brought your attention to the content once in a while, it is likely even after a cursory glance, you will be thinking…

- My hair is not long or thick enough
- My nails are not strong or long enough
- My lashes are not full enough

- My stomach is not flat enough
- My teeth are not white enough
- My skin is not smooth enough
- My skin is the wrong colour
- My nose is the wrong shape
- My lips are not full enough
- My boobs are too small and not pert enough
- I have too much cellulite
- I am the wrong weight, shape and my silhouette is ALL wrong

Add to this the pressure to lose your baby weight within weeks, be a yummy mummy, a vixen at work, a siren at home, a well-balanced career girl with domestic goddess tendencies, and a 'supermom' and it is not difficult to understand why so many of us are in the throes of an all-out identity crisis permanently! When did we become not enough?

he doesn't care that you are fat

As for what men want, most of them are bemused by our body battering. They want our feminine curves, our soft bodies, our vulnerabilities. Quite often they feel power-less to convince us of this with the backdrop I describe. Here is an excerpt from Eve Ensler's *The Good Body*. This is the transcript of a conversation she initiated with her partner after she had had an enlightened conversa-tion with a seventy-four-year old African Masai woman about whether she liked her body or not. The Masai woman's response is indignation at the thought of NOT loving her body, and she responds to Eve's plea, 'How do I do that, I want to love my body like you do, I hate my stomach!' by explaining that we are all meant to be different, just like trees. We do not dislike one tree or call it ugly because it is different from another. Eve reflects on this and does what many women do, she thinks out loud to her partner later on in the day and attempts to engage him as the third person in the conversation he was not party to. Here it is…

Eve – Honey, do you love my tree?

Partner – Every leaf, babe.

Eve – Huh. I didn't see leaves.

Partner – Yes, leaves and a solid trunk.

Eve – Solid… trunk?

Partner – Yes, solid, sturdy, trunk.

Eve – Sturdy. There is nothing sexy about sturdy. Sturdy is like a brick house; sturdy is like a boulder.

Partner – No, no, no. Sturdy is here. Sturdy is present. Sturdy turns me on.

Eve – Trees are willowy. I was going for willowy.

Partner – But you're athletic, Eve, you're strong. Full.

Eve – Full. Are you saying I am fat?

Partner – No, full like fit, like sturdy.

Eve – You just said I was fat.

Partner – I thought you were a tree, Eve? Trees aren't fat. I thought we were dealing with a tree?

Eve – Tree is gone. You chopped down tree. Now I'm a broken shrub.

Partner – I didn't chop down tree. Tree was clearly never really here. I am sick of your stomach, your shrub, your trunk, your stump, whatever it is. I can never get it right. I don't have an issue with your stomach. I have an issue with you. You're not here. I want a relationship with Eve. I am not going to compete with your stomach anymore.

Eve Ensler, The Good Body

Do you see what impossible situations our body insecurities create for the men that love us? They don't care if we have a tummy or cellulite (most would not even be able to point to cellulite if their life depended on it!), they would not even notice if we put on a few pounds, or stones in some cases, and I challenge you to evoke even a millisecond of recognition on the subject of orange peel skin!

They are bemused by our rants and simply have no idea what to say to us when we cry over our lumpy thighs or flat bottom! One of my favourite films is *The Birdcage* with talented Robin Williams and Nathan Lane as the gay couple who are continually bickering. Lane plays the lovable drama- and drag-queen Albert, who feels the club owner and his partner Armand, played by Williams, does not appreciate him/her. In an early scene just before Albert is due on stage for his nightly performance a disagreement breaks out focused on Albert's low self-esteem and he yells at a rather ambivalent Armand, 'I am hideous, I am in so much pain, I never used to be like this, I was adorable, gorgeous. Everything I am you made me – short, fat, insecure, a middle aged thing.' Armand looks shell-shocked and the only reply he can muster is: 'I made you short?' Classic!

What we interpret as imperfections, men cherish as our uniqueness and our vulnerability. They don't want to change this, they love this. They know it is unreal and impossible to look like a supermodel, their logic and common sense tells them this is fake – even the supermodels don't look like the magazine covers in the flesh. They care not a jot about this. And maybe, just maybe, they feel threatened by all this talk of perfection, because it may be their turn next? If you demand perfection in all things, what does that say about you?

Our body hang-ups are ours and ours alone. If we hate looking in the mirror and can say nothing positive about our reflection, it matters not what he says in return, we simply do not believe him, do not want to believe him. We think he has an agenda, does not care or is humouring or deluding us.

We need to step up and own this issue. We need to find our courage, our voice and inner strength to stop disfiguring our authenticity and stop feeding our insecurities with hate, drugs, surgery, addictions, obsessions, diseases and self-flagellation. Superwoman can only exist in this negative vacuum: once we fall back in love with ourselves, she will be powerless and the cape will disappear in a puff of smoke!

> To love oneself is the beginning of a lifelong romance.
>
> *Oscar Wilde*

the 'barbie doll' beauty generation

The pressure to conform to the 'Barbie doll' beauty ideal has been fuelled by the beauty industry for decades, but now – particularly in the past 10 years, as we have welcomed images of women as portrayed in porn as empowering and the sex industry has gone mainstream – a more serious, aggressive player has entered the market for our hearts and souls: cosmetic surgery. From Botox to total body lifts, we are bombarded by adverts telling us we really can be perfect, it's a modern-day miracle and our right! All of this is simply chipping away at our self-esteem, with our permission, or so it seems to me. We talk about lap dancing, pole dancing and burlesque as being empowering, we idolise WAGs, glamour models and porn stars, and we belittle and insult professional and powerful women and bully young girls who refuse to buy into this doll-like version of beauty. Whatever happened to sisterhood?

Now, don't get me wrong, I am all for a little enhance-
ment – I see nothing wrong in working with what you've
got – but this need to re-invent and distort our natural
beauty beyond make-up and traditional female adorn-
ments is a little worrying, and cannot be sending positive messages to our young girls.

Jordan, the poster girl of the 'Barbie doll' generation,
is still idolised by young girls. She is still one of the
most talked-about and admired role models for girls
aged 13-16 in UK schools. How scary is this? Here is
a woman who is clearly unwell, suffering with serious
body dysmorphia, addicted to surgery, insecure, in
need of constant validation via the press and her public
to bolster her delicate ego, and whose personal life,
which she chooses to share worldwide via every media
channel available, is hardly the stuff of dreams!

Regardless of how rich she is, or how entrepreneurial
she is, or how attentive a mother she is – is this who we
want our daughters to emulate? She is now followed
closely by Kim Kardashian as a role model of choice for
12-14 year olds, not an improvement in my book.

the facts are almost unbearable – can you join up the dots?

Now I am not about to go all academic on you, it was
never my intention to present a thesis on female empowerment through the ages, but I think it is important to

deal with some uncomfortable facts about our position TODAY, head on. We are living in dangerous times, particularly if you are female. We make up 70% of the world's poorest citizens, we are starving through choice and lack of choice, we are subject to violence, pain, mutilation and death at the hands of those who profess to love us, and we are cutting, slicing, sucking and scarring ourselves to achieve a deluded version of perfection that is quite simply insane and unattainable. In Africa, being born a girl means you are more likely to get raped than learn to read. In China, being born a girl increases your chances of being trafficked as boys are prized in a nation where a single child policy is favoured. If you are a girl conceived in India you are lucky even to be born, as an illegal dowry system makes you unaffordable and dispensable, and you are just as likely to end up a discarded foetus at the bottom of a disused well.[3]

I could go on, but I hope you get the message. I have my own opinions on our plight, but it is not my goal to preach or convert any of you to my way of thinking. I simply wish to present some facts and statements to you in order for you to join the dots in your own way. My only wish is that we wake up from sleepy denial sometime soon. If any of this encourages you to find out more, great: you will find a list of resources at the back of the book. I am not an expert nor an academic in the

---

[3] UN Children's Fund, *The State of the World's Children*, 2007

areas of female emancipation, mutilation or subjugation but I have read many publications and studies by the men and women who are and I respect them and their efforts to open our eyes and hearts to the global issues.

Here are some facts to get you thinking about what is really going on... It is not easy reading and I would ask you to consider the how and why of the facts I present. Do we really have equality and respect? Does the sex industry exploit us or empower us? What does liberation mean to our young girls? Where does the need to inflict pain and disfigure ourselves come from? Could there be a link between the normalisation of pornography and the increase in domestic violence? Why are rape convictions so low? You decide...

take a deep breath...

- There are now more lap dancing clubs (over 300) in the UK than rape crisis centres (only 38).

- In 2009 the Equality and Human Rights Commission threatened over 100 councils with legal action because they were failing to provide domestic violence support services or rape crisis centres, despite a growth in incidents reported.

- Half of all female murder victims worldwide are killed by a current or former partner. One in four women in the UK will experience domestic violence at some point in her life with two women murdered every week by a partner or former partner as a direct result.

- Surveys carried out in both the UK and the United States during the past 10 years report very high incidents of physical and sexual abuse, sometimes as high as 100%, towards women working in lap dancing and similar clubs. These women are openly disrespected, exploited, abused and treated with hostility and contempt, with very few of the perpetrators suffering ANY consequences.

- 25% of all daily search engine requests are for pornography. 96% of the people doing the searching are male. Every 39 minutes a new pornography video is created in the USA to support this demand. The industry is worth over $97 billion worldwide, more than the combined revenue of Microsoft, Google, Amazon, Yahoo!, Ebay, Apple, Netflix and Earthlink.

- Global prostitution is growing fast. During the 1990s the number of men paying for sex acts in the UK doubled. In 2008 there were at least 921 brothels in London alone.

- Between 600,000 and 800,000 people, 90% of them women and girls, are trafficked across national borders every year. Women and girls are trafficked primarily to service the multi-billion-dollar commercial sex industry, and modest estimates put the income generated by this relatively easy crime at $19 billion a year.

- Between 100 and 140 million of the world's female population have undergone female genital mutilation (FGM), including 6,000 women and girls living in the UK.

- Between 1992 and 2002 the number of people undergoing elective cosmetic surgery in the USA increased by 1600%. Over 90% of them were female. The UK is following the same trend. The most popular procedure in both countries is breast implants. The latest addition to the menu is the 'Designer Vagina', where women elect to have invasive procedures not dissimilar in nature and risk to those involved in FGM. Options include vaginal tightening, liposuction and lifting of lips, clipping of elongated inner lips and 'repair' of the hymen. (Are we saying that once the hymen is broken, i.e. when we lose our virginity, we are somehow damaged goods?)

- Up to 70 million people globally, mostly women, suffer from an eating disorder, and 1.5 million of these are in the UK. These disorders are among the top four causes of premature death, illness and disability amongst women aged 15-24 years old. 10% of women with anorexia die from it.

- 94% of all women's magazines have a picture of a model or celebrity on their front cover that would be considered thin, if not clinically underweight. The average model is now thinner than 98% of the female population. The average dress size in the UK is 16, yet a size 12 model is considered plus size. Not surprisingly, women are more than ten times more likely to have issues with their weight than men. In the UK we spend over £11 billion a year on books, magazines, special foods, classes and other aids to weight loss. 95% of all dieters regain all the weight they have lost.

- A survey in the UK in 2009 by Youngpoll.com found that a quarter of the 3,000 teenage girls questioned believed it was more important to be beautiful than clever.

- The Lab surveyed 1,000 15-19 year old girls in 2005 about their ambitions. 63% said they would rather be a nude or semi-nude glamour model than a nurse, a doctor or a teacher.

- In 2007, three French men developed an online gaming site for 9-16 year old girls, called **www. missbimbo.com.** It is positioned as an educational tool and is growing at a rate of 5,000 new members a day. Members create a bimbo character then earn bimbo dollars by challenging other bimbos and can spend their dollars on, amongst other items, nightclub outfits, plastic surgery, a psychologist and diet pills. Bimbos earn more points for maintaining a weight of 127 pounds, bagging a rich boyfriend and being popular. The aim of the game is for members to create the coolest, richest and most famous bimbo in the world. The top bimbo promoted and endorsed on the site is Paris Hilton.

- A recent study by The Samaritans states 1 in 10 teenagers self-harm, with four times as many girls as boys cutting and self-mutilating. Because of the secrecy involved in this act, experts suggest the real figure is closer to 1 in 4 girls, the same ratio for the number of girls under the age of 16 on a diet.

I know all of this is tough to absorb and some of you may be saying, 'So what?'... I have no answer to that response, but for the rest of us...

I genuinely believe we can have it all, whatever ALL means to you, but we need to get real about where our expectations are coming from, and adjust our view of unattainable perfectionism accordingly. It is time to face some harsh facts about the equality illusion and get angry about the global treatment of women. This includes waking up to the reality of the negative impact the mainstreaming of the sex industry is having on our culture and next generation. I LOVE being a woman and I feel confident that we will unite in sisterhood to escape from the living doll culture that is professing to be our salvation. Empowerment comes in many guises but, in my opinion, it cannot be found whilst dancing around a pole, half nude, regardless of how this is mis-sold, nor does it wear a cape and a badge saying invincible.

Our pioneering days are not over yet, ladies, so let me introduce you to the new superwoman...

introducing the all new, supercharged, superwoman of the 21st century

strong woman syndrome© - the stickability of superwoman

Working with a diverse group of women over the past decade has given me access to the mindset of working women and the opportunity to spot some trends in their behaviour. In response to what I have seen, a couple of years ago I developed a behaviour model called *Strong Woman Syndrome©*. Women displaying the behaviour traits of this model are perfectionists. They have very high expectations of themselves – they have to be the best mother, best boss, best team player, best social host, best lover, best daughter, best neighbour, best sister, best domestic goddess, best wife, best best friend and so on. Oh, and they have to subscribe to the media's position on beauty at the same time so alongside being the best, they have to look perfect doing it! So an exorbitant amount of time and money is spent on how they look, dress, smell, walk etc.

And as this self-imposed perfectionism is totally impossible to sustain, when they fail to deliver, or fall off this self-built pedestal for even a minute, they are the first to beat themselves up for the smallest of misdemeanours! Late to pick up Johnny from school, burn the tea, forget to Sky plus husband's favourite show, so exhausted by Friday night they order a takeaway? Bad mother! The big wins they may have achieved at work are disregarded, at this point it's all the other stuff they feel intense guilt about.

Because they have such high expectations of themselves and high standards, they believe the people around them have pretty low expectations because no one can do anything as well as them. (Why would they want to?) They will say things like, 'You just can't get the staff', or 'By the time I've shown you how to do this I could have done it myself', or 'No-one else can do this like me, it's easier and faster to do it myself than show someone else.'

So they end up controlling the whole show, at home and at work. It's their way or no way. This turns them into quite intimidating, scary control freaks! Women stuck here tend to complain a lot about lack of work/life balance, they talk about juggling and doing everything and being exhausted with no 'me' time. Know any??

This model of behaviour is very hard to sustain. Juggling can only ever be a temporary state so it's not long before a plate or two comes crashing to the floor and things go wrong. But guess what? When this happens strong women simply blame everyone else! It cannot possibly be their fault, remember, they are doing everything! And all you personal development junkies know only too well that if you blame everyone else for your life decisions and choices, that makes you a VICTIM. Interestingly, this is a position of weakness, not strength. So all this time we think we are projecting a strong, in-control woman, underneath we are weak and vulnerable, the two states we fear most.

This is a very confusing model of behaviour. We switch from superwoman to victim continuously, sometimes several times a day or even in the duration of a conversation, and we wonder why we are misunderstood. One minute we are in total control, invincible and strutting along in our high heels, the next minute we are a bumbling wreck of insecurities, blaming the world for our plight, feeling unloved and unappreciated and exhausted!

> *'I realised after 8 years of running my own business and raising two children that my strive for perfection in all areas was having a really negative impact on my health, sanity and my relationships. I finally decided to bite the bullet and get a cleaner to take care of the house and even asked my mum for her help when it came to the ironing! I actually managed to ask my husband for help which he gave willingly and, despite the fact that it goes against my nature, I have a much happier household and a more balanced life – being superwoman isn't all it's cracked up to be!'*
>
> *Claire, married mother of 2 running a PR company*

can you wash up please, love...?

Here is an example of a scenario played out in thousands of households every night...

You and your partner/husband etc have both arrived home after a day at work. You make the dinner and ask him to wash up. He dutifully embraces the task and after a reasonable amount of time has elapsed you arrive in the kitchen for your inspection...

At this point you call him back to the scene of the crime and say, 'I thought I asked you to wash up?' He looks perplexed and replies, 'Well, I have.' Now you take a deep breath, stand tall and produce your evidence. 'Oh, you have? Really? Well, you have not swept the floor, emptied the bin, wiped down the worktops or used the special cloth to get rid of all the smears on our stainless steel appliances. You have loaded the dishwasher incorrectly and the casserole dish is still on the hob. And in all the time we have lived together, when have you ever seen me put crystal glasses in the dishwasher?'

He generally only has two standard replies to this outburst:

1. Well, you never asked me to do all of that, you just asked me to wash up and I did!

2. Well, you know what to do next time then: do it yourself!

Thing is, our reply to this rebuff is generally along the lines of 'Right, well I'll do it myself then, like I do everything else around here anyway. Pathetic, if you want a job doing right in this house, you have to do it yourself blah blah blah!'

Ring any bells? This is an example of Strong Woman Syndrome© in action. We demand everything be done to our standards, we control the show, we, in effect, disempower everyone else, then get upset when it goes wrong or does not meet our exacting standards.

Now, before you start screaming at me, let's talk some more about this.

I know most men are useless in the kitchen or with many domestic tasks. A very good friend of mine coined the term 'domestic dyslexia' in relation to men and I love this! I also know most men want to do whatever is necessary to make us happy. It is just that the two do not always coincide. Incidentally I am pretty useless looking after my car, the garden, any equipment/machinery, making fires, fixing stuff and/or heavy lifting. My husband does all of this unprompted and without complaint and he never asks me to participate or learn any of it! Maybe we should recognise each other's strengths rather than demand we become interchangeable! Just a thought…

It is almost impossible to change other people, particularly men. We can only change ourselves. But magical things happen when we do change. Our shift creates a tidal wave around us and is a catalyst for different behaviour in others too.

Be the change you want to see in the world

Ghandi

We all display some Strong Woman tendencies, and this is manageable and part of our charm, but if you control everything in your house and beyond – the budget, the cleaning regime, where you eat, shop, holiday, who does what, when, how and where; if you choose your joint friends, regulate conversations, choose your husband's clothes, what he can and cannot eat – in effect, if you control the whole show, be warned: this is a recipe for relationship conflict, emotional pain and not an ideal life model to pass on!

How about this comment from a male coaching client of mine, convinced he was having a midlife crisis and suffering with seriously low self-esteem:

> *'I am not allowed to eat pies and there's no point trying to sneak one in 'cos my wife always smells my clothes for evidence when I get home and it's not worth the nagging followed by the silent treatment if I disobey her.'*

a disempowered man is an unhappy man...

Although I recognise and understand you may feel you have been driven here and have no choice, there is always a choice. If you are controlling, you are disempowering your partner and a disempowered man is not a happy man. He generally has two choices in response to being totally controlled:

- He can accept this and sit back and let you get on with it, bearing with apathy your nagging and inevitable outbursts. But this seriously affects his spirit, confidence and self-esteem.

- Or he can step up and attempt to gain back some control, but unfortunately this will not be in the areas you want. He will not be fighting with you as to who cleans the kitchen, negotiates with the nanny or does the weekly food shop.

Some women work so hard to make good husbands that they never manage to make good wives.

Neither option gives you what you want and need, but you do control the outcome. Learning to let go of some of this controlling is the essence of this book. It does require a shift in mindset and some behaviour and belief reframes. As you let go and surrender your control amazing things will happen – I promise!

The Strong Woman behaviour model, also known as New Superwoman, appears to be a position of strength but in reality it is a place of weakness. Controlling everything does not give you power, it gives you an almighty headache! It is emotionally exhausting to think that the only way to demand respect, or to be loved, or to be needed is to DO everything, for everyone, perfectly. What would happen if you let go? What would happen if you made mistakes every now and again? What would happen if the kitchen were NOT spotless every night? What would happen if you allowed others to help, plan, do? You see? Too often we are playing the Strong Woman role at home AND in work. We work late, without any recognition, because we want the task to be perfect; we control projects at a micro level because we do not trust anyone else to do it to our standards, and this keeps us stuck at middle management level;

we never delegate or consider employing staff in our own business because no-one does it better than us and you simply cannot get the staff anyway, everyone knows that – it's a universal truth if you are superwoman!

The crux of this behaviour model is around energy, and superwoman spends most of her day in her male energy. This is not natural, it distorts her natural dynamic, and therefore is tough to sustain.

> *The only thing worse than a man you can't control, is a man you can.*

> **Margo Kaufman**

let's talk about energy....

Both men and women have male and female energy. What is important to understand is that both energies are very different. Men and women are designed to be different but complementary. When we spend too much time in each other's energy we lose our authenticity and the relationship dynamic is knocked out of its natural balance. This happens in all situations – at home and in the workplace.

It is clear to see that at some time we both need to access all these energy traits, regardless of our gender. However, the key is about where you choose to live and your authenticity. I am a strong, sassy, success-ful woman. Often I need my male energy, particularly in business, but it is not where I live. I embrace my feminine side. It is my natural position. It is where my power is. I delight in my emotional, intuitive response to life.

FEMALE ENERGY TRAITS	MALE ENERGY TRAITS
Nurturing	Competitive
Passive – need for peace and harmony	Aggressive – fight mentality ready, if needed
Multi-task/think and process	Task-orientated/single-minded focus
Sees big picture, global thinker	Compartmentalised thinker
Emotional and compassionate	Power/rank status is key
Supportive and team orientated	Strong on productivity and practical
Focus on value and meanings	Focus on facts/reason/logic
Open and vulnerable	Protective
Creator – happy to create space for others to grow	Provider – need to fix and solve
Receptive, intuitive and gentle	Linear, direct and action orientation
EXERTS POWER THROUGH ATTRACTION	EXERTS POWER THROUGH CONTROL

In order to be whole, a man needs to have a connection with his poetic, nurturing, gentle and creative feminine side. If he did not access this as some point, he would not be able to emotionally connect with you, his life partner, nor would he be able to develop a loving relationship with his children. However, be clear, it is not his primary energy.

Conversely a woman, in order to be whole, needs to have a connection with her strong, achieving, productive, focused masculine side. Without this she would not capitalise on her talents at work or in her business. She needs to step up and be assertive on many occasions and this is where she taps into her male energy. However, be clear, it is not her primary energy.

This energy chart almost always causes debate amongst professional, modern women. The insinuation that they may sometimes be vulnerable and passive causes an outcry! But we must be careful with our interpretation of words here…

When I say passive, I do not mean weak. In energy terms, we are defining a woman's response to conflict. He will step up, be aggressive and fight. She will want to calm the situation, be passive and talk. I am in this position several times a week with my husband! He is the archetypal Alpha male, ex-police, ex-United Nations, ex-action-hero type. If I were not grounded in my female energy, I would not have attracted him, nor would I be able to love him! I often wonder: if we had more women in politics and the military, how often might physical conflict be avoided in exchange for a more passive approach to a resolution?

I will deal with the vulnerability debate in a later chapter
– it is a biggy!

In her book *The Essence of Womanhood – Re-Awakening
the Authentic Feminine,* Susie Heath's list of female attri-
butes includes:

> *Sensual, loving, warm, dark, passionate, like juicy fruit,
> wild, seductive, tender, powerful, curvaceous, moist,
> compassionate, flexible, delicious, surrendering, intui-
> tive, emotional, deep, connecting, like a flower bud, ca-
> ressing, secret, smouldering, honouring life, reliable, de-
> pendable, truthful, earthy, voluptuous, sexy, soft, open,
> embracing, fluid, bowing and bending, seeking equilib-
> rium, beautiful, thoughtful, funny, with a quiet, hidden
> nurturing side that is at the centre of her feminine na-
> ture. And yet at the same time, she can be mischievous,
> childlike, frivolous, petulant, saucy, wilful, playful, one
> moment a harlot, the next moment the lover, teacher,
> the healer, the mother.*

Back to Strong Woman Syndrome©. When I talk to
successful, career/professional women about this
model of behaviour, initially they are a tad defensive
as they interpret the model as a personal affront. They
feel they have been forced to step up because men are
useless and if you want to have it all, this is the way
it is. For me, this is a classic case of buying into the
hype, being sold the guilt trip that comes with a career
outside the home and the media's focus on perfection

and, importantly, attracting and disempowering the wrong man! However, after more discussion and some honesty around authenticity and energy, the real stress of keeping all the balls in the air and needing a real man to step up and share always come to the fore.

I have been running personal development workshops for women for the past seven years and every time I ask women to define their fears in keeping hold of this model of behaviour, one that works on the premise of control and perfectionism, where saying 'No' is perceived as a weakness and saying 'Yes' to help is unheard of, the answers and discussions always focus on...

the fear of letting go

They say...

- If I let go of control I may be found out. People will see I am not as clever/smart/sassy/together as I project. When I am found out, people will see that I am a fraud and the job I am doing is not all that difficult.
- If I do not do everything at home, nothing will get done and I will not be loved or needed.
- If I am not perfect, I am not deserving of love. Unless I am 100% focused on working it, I will uncover my insecurities and be seen as weak.
- If I ask for or accept help I will be seen as vulnerable, and vulnerable equals weak.

So, it would appear that the fear of not being enough or somehow being seen as weak keeps us locked into this destructive model of behaviour. When I carry on this discussion with women and ask them 'What do you have to believe about YOU to sustain this model?' these are the most common answers…

- No one is as capable as me. If I don't do it, it won't get done.
- If I do not keep all the balls in play, my life will fall apart.
- I am alone and fully responsible for the whole show and I always will be. (Closely followed by 'All the good men are either married or gay and the rest are just b******s.')
- Men and/or staff always let you down. It is far better to do everything yourself.
- Kids have no respect these days.
- It's all I deserve.

the conclusion is not pretty

Not very empowering is it? To think, over 100 years of liberation and in the 21st century this is where we are. I think we have lost our way a little. Surely this is not what our early pioneers meant by becoming a woman of independent means? How did we translate equality to this: beating ourselves up, people-pleasing to excess and self-sabotage?

Superwoman, she who is all controlling, she who would never display vulnerability, she who would never ask for help, she who would never say no – she is feeding our insecurities, she is damaging our self-belief, she is sabotaging our businesses and relationships and she is NOT a great life model to pass onto our young girls. It is time to let her go...

There is a better place to live. A more nourishing place, where you are allowed to embrace your vulnerability, in fact, where vulnerability is power. A place where you can be true to yourself and be loved for who you are, not what you do. A place where being female is a joy, where you can tap into your intuition, passion, emotions and love. A place where it is OK to cry, to ask for help, to say 'No' and to hand over control, sometimes!

In the following chapters of this book I will discuss the Strong Woman Syndrome© and Superwoman as they relate to the different roles and identities we all play at one time in our life. Many of us are playing several roles simultaneously so I suggest you read all the chapters as opposed to simply tapping into sections that at first glance appeal or relate to you most. This is because even though you may be married, some of the content I discuss in the chapter on being single may be relevant to you, eg the need for self-love. As you read, be honest with yourself. See how you are showing up and do what you have to do to let Superwoman go – it is time. We need to do this, our men need us to do this, our daughters need us to do this and the women of the world need us to do this NOW.

My antithesis to Superwoman is a Well Heeled Diva. This is a brand I established over seven years ago to support women to change and grow and we are now a national community on- and off-line. Women who participate in our personal development and entrepreneurial programmes are proud to call themselves Divas and this term has developed a life of its own! Our definition of a Diva has come to represent the ideal description of a sassy, strong woman who has given up on Superwoman and is living life to the max. I hope you like it and will step up and join us when you are ready. We are all 'works in progress'! You can read more about The Divas at the back of the book and you will see quotes from many Divas throughout the chapters.

Here is our mantra....

A Diva is a woman who knows who she is and loves herself. She knows what is important to her and what she wants. She embraces her female energy, lives with balance, love, passion and authenticity and is a role model to other women and young girls. She knows her greatness and shines.

'I have been playing the Strong Woman game for at least 12 years and the need to be in total control has cost me dearly. I lost the real me, I became a great, if deep down unhappy, actress.

Today I am learning that it is OK not to know the answers to everything, not to be perfect, not to make all the decisions etc. I am having GREAT fun re-discovering my inner girlie side, she has always been there, but I have not let her out to play for some time. I am now ready to create the space for a different life with a real man, and acknowledging this has been truly liberating.'

Carol, a Diva, divorced mother of 2 running her own business

One of the many roles women are playing in the Strong Woman portfolio is Supermom.

Supermom runs her household like a military operation. The fridge is covered with calendars, to-do lists, reminders, school schedules, shopping lists and coupons. Her work handbag would make the SAS jealous – it contains enough junk for any emergency and can withstand all weather conditions. In the film One Fine Day, super, single mom (an even more developed hybrid) manages to make a fancy dress outfit for her four-year-old son in three minutes flat using the contents of her handbag, on arrival at the school gates, which is when he remembered to inform her it was dress-up day!

Supermom can and does multi-task within an inch of total burnout daily and her schedule is planned with such precision it only takes an unexpected traffic holdup on the school run to require a total overhaul of the day and evening!

Her emotional state shifts from relief to guilt to panic with glimmers of joy and exhaustion every hour!

And as a working mum it is imperative that she looks perfect too. So high heels, make-up, perfect nails, hair and teeth and stylish clothes are also key. Yummy Mummy has got nothing on this babe. She can apply mascara in the rear view mirror whilst touching up her nails all on the journey to work.

So to summarise.... Supermom has to juggle a job with bringing up kids. She is sometimes married, but not always, she may employ the services of a nanny or housekeeper and she may be financially wealthy or not. The model is still intact regardless of the economic situation of the main player as most of the perfection-ist, impossible-to-reach-and-sustain standards are self-imposed.

We have become so accustomed to reading about the eternal search for a work/life balance and the need to juggle that we have accepted this as our lot. We some-how do not feel like we are doing our job or being a good mother unless we are rushing around at 90 miles an hour, clutching our to-do list, continually topping up our guilt and sacrificing any me-time for family time.

Not only is this not fun, it is not sensible. If you have ever travelled on a plane the air stewards deliver a very powerful lesson for Supermoms everywhere: 'In the event of decompression in the cabin, oxygen masks will drop from the overhead compartment. If you are travelling with children please place the oxygen mask over your own mouth as a priority, before securing theirs.' Interesting…. the message is clear, put yourself first, because if anything happens to you, your loved ones are at risk! Supermom does not live by this mantra – everyone else is more important than her, especially the kids. Supermom is over-protective, constantly fixing and rescuing and struggles to let go, controlling all her offspring's decisions well past the time when this is reasonable or helpful.

overprotecting leads to apathy

I am often amazed and disheartened when I speak to young people these days. Apathy seems to be a national disease. I work with teenagers all the time so I am well aware of the pressures of looming unemployment, aimless career direction, the rising costs for first-time buyers, peers, bullying, obsession with physical appearance etc, but mollycoddling them does not help. They have to find their own way, supported by the adults in their life not controlled by them. It saddens me to see so many adult children still living in the family home well into their twenties. Life begins at the end of your comfort zone and the longer they stay cocooned with no real responsibility or independence the tougher it will be to integrate, find peers, sustain relationships, develop emotional resilience and start living!

> *'Mum, I am hungry, when are you coming home?' – 16 year old.*

> *'Mum, I have no money and I need an outfit for Saturday night...' – 21 year old*

> *'Mum, I've just been to the cash machine and your cash card is not working, now what am I going to do?' – 14 year old*

> *'Mum, some of us are planning a trip to New York. I can sort my flight but you will have to pay for the rest.' – 26 year old*

I have overheard all these conversations and often struggled to stay quiet!

letting supermom go

Remember, a Diva is a woman who knows who she is and loves herself. She knows what is important to her and what she wants. She embraces her female energy, lives with balance, love, passion and authenticity and is a role model to other women and young girls. She knows her greatness and shines.

Stop fixing and rescuing. Everybody in the house is NOT your responsibility.

Teach self-sufficiency not co-dependency.

Encourage teens to think about independence and their own space. It is not healthy for your kids to still be living in your space well into their twenties, however hard life is – did you have it so easy?

Tough love sometimes is the only love.

Make time for play and chat.

If you are working full time or running a business, dump the guilt and get some help with the boring stuff like ironing, cleaning, shopping. Release yourself from the drudgery – what is the point of advancement if it does not make your life easier?

Simplify your schedule.

Accept help when it is offered regardless of where it comes from – mum-in-law, girlfriends, partner, PA – if you keep refusing, eventually they will stop offering and you will feel very alone, isolated and more at risk of a total meltdown.

Learn to say NO. It is very liberating! This applies to every facet of Strong Woman Syndrome. The need to be loved and needed seems to implant a microchip that can only respond with YES. Reprogram it today!

If your teenager's bedroom looks like a junkyard, simply shut the door and create a new rule – it must be cleaned by them weekly, no ifs and buts, no ultimatums, just fact.

Rules and boundaries – get some!

superwoman becomes superwife 4

For Superwife read wife, girlfriend, partner etc. Superwife is a formidable woman. She is a whirlwind of negative, fear-induced energy, creating panic and guilt wherever or on whatever she decides is her priority in the moment. I see them, in packs, strutting around every corner, issuing orders on their mobiles to their other halves. They live at the edge of their temper threshold most of the time. Any tiny misunderstanding or omission can lead to meltdown and the focus of most of their anger and frustration is directed at their husband/life partner.

men are just teenagers in disguise...

Superwife is controlling the whole show, but interestingly when challenged her defensive response is generally, 'Well, if I don't do everything around here, nothing would get done. He [husband] hasn't got a clue, never makes any decisions, is happy to leave it all up to me and most of the time behaves like one of the kids anyway!'

My response… You have created this scenario. If he behaves like a teenager, you have taught him how to do that and allowing this behaviour to continue unchecked tells him it is OK. Passing the blame on is acting like a victim again and will keep you stuck. Step up and take some responsibility for how things are today and decide to behave differently.

Here is a classic relayed to me by a seriously henpecked and controlled husband in a coaching session. I was facilitating a goal-setting exercise and part of his input was to share his dream board with his wife. This is how the conversation unfolded at his home…

'So, John,' his wife enquired, 'What does your dream house look like?'

John replied: 'Oh, not entirely sure, but it is overlooking the beach, somewhere tropical like the Caribbean.'

His wife sighed, took a property factsheet from their local estate agents out of her handbag, thrust it at him and replied 'Oh for God's sake John, let's be practical, it has to be on the bloody school run, here it is, now stick this picture on your goal board.'

This simple conversation told me all I needed to know about his marital relationship. It was HIS goal board, yet she controlled the conversation from point one asking him about his dream house as opposed to listening to him share his dreams with her. Remember, it was HIS process. Then she spoke to him like a naughty child and proceeded to tell him what his dream house looked like and where it was! John is a typical example of a disempowered man. He was very unhappy in his marriage but loved his wife; he really wanted it all to work but had no idea how to get his wife to back off without upsetting her and his self-esteem was at an all-time low, hence him turning to coaching.

This is an extreme example, but I would guess this banter is being repeated in the homes of many professional working couples. The role boundaries have blurred and both sides are struggling to understand the needs of the other.

change is personal, it is not your gift to your husband!

It is important for ALL of us to understand we cannot change anyone else, particularly our men. We can only be responsible for ourselves. We spend far too much time trying and failing to change our men from the minute we meet them and we need to stop. The more we nag, the more they rebel.

We need an honest review of the situation and this comes back to universal needs and energy. This may be an uncomfortable discussion for some of you but I ask that you keep an open mind and stay with me for a while...

fact – our needs are different – oh yeah!

A loved-up couple may share a passion for good food, the outdoors and family time. They may reside in the same house, go on the same holidays, even work together in the same company, but their needs are different and this will show up in their attitude, values, behaviour and beliefs.

At a base level we both need to feel valued, loved, respected and special but our expectations on how these needs are met is gender dependent. There, I have said it – phew! Just wait a moment... OK, I have not been struck by lightening or disappeared in a puff of smoke, so maybe I can carry on?

the universal needs

HE NEEDS	SHE NEEDS
ACKNOWLEDGEMENT & APPRECIATION	CERTAINTY
ADMIRATION	CHERISHING & COMPLIMENTING
AWAY TIME	COMMUNICATION

Let's talk about the guys....

men need you to invest in their ego

It's all about managing that delicate male ego. They need to know you are proud of them, you need them, you are impressed by their prowess (whatever that is!) and that you trust them to protect you, your shared environment and your family. The very worst thing you can say to a man is 'I do not need you'. Which is, inter-estingly, a comment I hear time and time again from superwomen everywhere.

So let's dig a little deeper – stay with me:

Acknowledged

He needs to know that you value his wisdom, his prow-ess, his input. Men want to fix things, they want to make us happy, they want and need love as much as we do. He needs to be able to share his knowledge with you, unfortunately this often translates into fixing and then we shift into defensive mode and it all goes wrong. Allow me to share what happens in my household…

Tony and I have been together for 15 years. He is a wise man, has lived a full and interesting life, is well travelled, well read and well hard! In the early stages of our rela-tionship I would continually lose it with him as he tried to fix me! I would share an event in my day and before I had even finished the story he would be fixing me: 'Well, you know what you want to do? You want to tell him,

and show her, and change this and move that, etc, etc.'
This got me so angry as I was not looking for his opinion,
I simply needed to let off some steam, talk, share, come
down after a tense meeting or situation. Ring any bells?
The result was confusion on both parts. He was only
trying to help and support me and I was getting wound
up as I felt undermined and patronised. After some soul
searching and because we love each other and hated
causing each other pain, we got it and created a new
behaviour pattern that satisfies both of our needs. You
see, I know Tony is wise, his energy and skillset are
totally different to mine and as such very valuable to me
as an entrepreneur and often I seek his opinion, but it is
almost impossible for him to know when I am asking for
this and when I just need to be heard.

So, we have a system and it works MOST of the time.
If I am looking for his opinion, I ask for it. Otherwise,
he knows I am just letting off steam, and I need him to
actively listen to me and support me without fixing.

In this way he is acknowledged. He knows what I need
as opposed to having to mind read. He knows I recognize his value and need his input in my life. He is happy.

Appreciated
He needs to feel the love! He needs to know he is not
simply on board for the ride, regardless of how exciting the ride is! When he grasps the initiative, makes a
decision – even something as simple as choosing the
restaurant or calling into the farm shop on the way

home – the power of 'Thank you, darling' can be pretty awesome!

Most of the time this appreciation shows itself in a multitude of ways that you will not even be consciously aware of if your energy is aligned. When I asked my husband how he feels appreciated these are most of his replies (some I was not prepared to share!):

> *'Making my favourite dinner, baking, wearing colours and outfits you know I love, helping me organise my office [a never ending task I can assure you!], buying me little gifts when I least expect them like a book, some liquorice or a DVD, sharing your day with me, setting Sky Plus to record one of my favourite TV shows when I have forgotten, telling me how much you appreciate me, my input etc. Most of the time just knowing your day is richer because I am in it is all I need to hear!'*

Ahhh, bless, eh? But it is so simple to do this if you love someone. And before you rant, 'Well, he does nothing anyway', I defy any of you to not be able to acknowledge and appreciate at least one thing every day – just do it, the results are worth it.

Admired

This need is grounded in that male pride we all know so well. He needs to know you are proud of him, you admire him and respect his male gallantry, his masculinity. This is not about recognizing he can colour co-ordinate his shirt and tie or that he is a good golfer. It is primal. He needs to know that you recognize his ability to care for and protect you and your family, that he is doing a good job, meeting your needs. He needs to know you see him as a strong, powerful man, in control of his environment and his role in it. When I asked Tony to share how he feels admired in our relationship this was the one he had most difficulty articulating. You see, as with most things in life, when it works, it just does and deconstructing the 'how' takes some time and thought. However, he is in no doubt that I do admire him, he has just never had to think about it! Having had a few days to reflect on this here is his answer…

> *'When I overhear Jane talking about me to other women, when she describes me as wise, well-travelled etc, I can literally feel this as a physical sensation – I stand taller, I feel more confident and alive and I positively preen! It can be a certain look that melts me or a throwaway comment like 'I know you will know the answer to this, Tony…' or, 'Give me your perspective on this babe…'*

> *It is a certain knowing; Jane often pre-empts my reaction to many situations, she knows who I am in my soul and good or bad she knows how to manage my aggressive male tendencies with ease. She does this in such a way that I know she admires this about me, it is hard to define but I know she wants me to be the man and therefore I am free to live in my natural place. She encourages me to be authentic, she validates me. She so gets the best of me. In the words of Jack Nicholson*

in the film As Good As It Gets – 'She makes me want to be a better man!"

On a recent trip out together I was struck by another example of this. Tony started his career as a police officer in a quaint village in North Wales, the archetypal 'village bobby'. He has recently written a crime novel based on his career in the police and was keen to go back to this village where it all began. It was the most stunning, picturesque, quaint village I have ever seen, nestling in a valley, cocooned by fragrant fir trees and every hue of green. The population of the village was only 1,000 and everyone knew each other and was part of each other's lives. The police officer was the pillar of the community, respected and revered. Tony was married with a young child at this time and as we sat outside the building that used to be his police station and his home (now just a house) I said, 'You know, babe, I really wish I had lived here with you, it is so peaceful and the sense of community so strong. I wonder how our life would be different now if we had met when we were young?'

Tony's response was heart-wrenching: 'I know for sure that if you would have been with me during my career in the force I would definitely have ended up the Chief Constable [the highest ranking officer in the force].' When I asked him to explain why, he continued, 'Well, I want you to be proud of me and I know that with your support, encouragement and love I would have flown up the ranks.'

This is an example of what I am saying in action. Tony knows I admire and respect him and I want him to shine, because when he shines, I shine and vice versa.

Again some of you may be saying, 'Well, that's all well and good, but my husband does nothing worthy of my admiration anyway – he does not provide or protect, he sits around all day, whilst I earn the money, he does not help around the house, he has no pride.' Well, how did that happen? How did you get to this point? This book is not a strategy for relationship rescue; if you are experiencing serious breakdown in your communications, values and contribution maybe reading a few books is not enough? Step up with courage – you both deserve to be happy, if you have love you will have the desire to make it right.

> 'Do you know how good you make a man feel when you let him know he makes a difference in your life? And do you know how good you will feel when you see his face come alive with joy in being reminded that he does, indeed make a difference?'
>
> From Susan Jeffers in her book *Opening Our Hearts to Men*

Away Time

Men need space and solitude on a regular basis. They need a place of their own to get away from you, the kids, work and life. This is not personal, it does not mean they are unhappy or working on an escape plan! They just need time to retire to their cave every now and again. This cave can take many forms – the shed, the greenhouse and/or garden, the garage or their own room. Tony has his own den in our home. It is his place and I very rarely venture into it. It is his office//TV room/chill-out zone/store room and thinking space. It is where he surrounds himself with his stuff, his books and films, his treasured native Indian chest plates and headdresses, his military history memorabilia and his police collections. It is a mystery to me how he ever finds anything, writes or relaxes amidst such chaos and to say it is untidy is an understatement but I do not touch anything unless I have permission and I respect his privacy.

But this is only one aspect of his away time. Most guys develop hobbies, sport interests and activities outside of work. This is a way of channelling their aggression, competitive nature and/or creating some male bonding time. Superwoman tends not to appreciate this and gets very agitated when he is on the golf course and she is left to do ALL the work but here is the thing… You need this time out/me time too. Just because you are prepared to sacrifice it in order to control the whole show does not mean he should too. You cannot control him and he cannot control you. Two exhausted control freaks do not a happy couple make! If you are berating him for his away time, maybe you are neglecting your own?

So what about us? What do we need in return for all this admiration, acknowledgement and appreciation?

women need to be seen and heard

What do women want? This has become the holy grail of all relationship debates, the storyboard of a multitude of TV sitcoms and stand up routines, it has spawned a plethora of self-help books and is one of the most talked-about subjects on the dinner party circuit, but if we are really honest with ourselves we are not that complicated, are we?

Let's get back to basics, because it's a lack of focus on basics that has led us to this point. Role boundaries have blurred, our identities are confused, we are single mothers attempting to take on the role of two parents, we are working mums attempting to play hardball at work and switching heads on the journey home to become nurturing mum and (if you're lucky) adoring wife! Spinning and juggling has created confusion, competing with men at work has violated our female energy and values and we now feel, in some cases demand, the same needs as men have AND our own! We want to be appreciated, adored and admired too. Or do we? Do we really? Do you want to be admired for your wisdom, ability to fight and aggression? Do you want to be acknowledged for your logical, linear viewpoint and single task focus? Maybe you do, but is this your primary need? I am not convinced. I just think we are confused and reacting to the constant kickbacks of thriving as women in a patriarchal society. Like it or not it is still a man's world. We may have been emancipated and given access to the world of work, but we are still paid less, earn less pension, work longer hours, are subject to ongoing harassment and inequality and as a result have access to less advancement than men for the privilege. Our pioneering days are still ahead of us, and if in doubt read on...

- Women do two thirds of the world's work, yet receive 10 per cent of the world's income and own only 1 per cent of the means of production.[4]
- The gender pay gap in the UK is currently 19.1% and widening.[5]
- 30,000 women are sacked each year in the UK simply for being pregnant.[6]
- Women make up only 12% of FTSE 100 company directors and there are still 25 of these companies with no women on their board at all.[7]
- The total proportion of female directors across all companies decreased from 43% in 1991 to 34% in 2007 and it continues to drop.[8]

---

[4] Richard H. Robins, *Global Problems and the Culture of Capitalism* (Allyn & Bacon, 1999)
[5] THE TIME TO ACT IS NOW: Fawcett's Gender Pay Gap Briefing, November 2014
[6] Equal Opportunities Commission report, 2005
[7] The Equalities Review, 2007
[8] The Equalities Review, 2007

- Women still dominate the lowest paid occupations, in particular the five Cs: cleaning, caring, clerical work, cashiering and catering.[9]
- The mother's low income is the source of 70% of child poverty in the UK. A third of the children of single parents (9 out of 10 single parents are women) live in poverty.[10]
- A recent study carried out by the European Commission reported that exposure to sexual harassment could be as high as 70-90% in the workplace.
- TopTenREVIEWS reported in 2007 that 20% of men admitted accessing pornography at work.
- Less than 20% of MPs in the UK are women. This dropped even further in recent elections (2010).

Makes you think, eh?

So, back to our needs...

Our universal needs are to have certainty, be cherished/loved and complimented and have communication. Convinced? Let's take a closer look and remember these are your needs in your relationship.

Certainty
Certainty is absolute faith and certainty that your husband/partner/man will look out for you, will be

---

[9] The Fawcett Society, 2013
[10] The Fawcett Society, 2013

there, will do what is necessary to provide, protect and support you and your family.

It is an unspoken truth, a knowing that makes you feel secure and loved.

It is not related to who earns what, who is or is not the breadwinner. It is more basic than that. It is focused on the BIG picture not the minutiae of everyday life decisions.

Many years ago I attended a personal development evening where the speakers were husband and wife team Nicki and Tony Vee and they spoke about some of these universal needs as a taster to their relationship retreats. The way they defined certainty made perfect sense to me. Enter the dragon...

enter the dragon – let natural order be restored

Let's say you and your husband are in a room and a dragon enters. (Stay with me here.) You both recognize the danger immediately but there are 3 possible responses to this situation:

1. you push your husband out of the way, preferably behind you, so you can take control and sort it.

2. as the dragon enters your husband turns to you and asks, 'Do you want to get this or shall I?'

3. as the dragon enters the room your husband steps in front of you so you are completely hidden and out of immediate danger and proceeds to deal with the problem.

Now, options 1 and 3 give you certainty. Option 1 is you taking control, stepping into your male energy and saying, 'I am OK, I can handle this, I do not need a man, he is useless anyway, better to rely on myself.' There is certainty for you but you have in fact disempowered him, which will lead to relationship conflict in the long term; as I discussed earlier, a disempowered man is not a happy man and this model is not a long-term bet.

Option 3 also gives you certainty. Here you feel safe and secure in the knowledge that your man is there for you, you do not have to do everything, he will step up and protect you when he needs to. You are not alone. This is a natural position for him and he is totally empowered, in his male energy and rocking! The knock-on effect of this is that you are allowed to embrace your female energy and let go of Superwoman. A win/win situation.

Now let's talk about option 2, where he turns to you and requests a debate. This makes you feel totally uncertain and generally results in you losing faith in his ability to do anything, so you take over, step up to control the whole show, feeling frustrated, disappointed and resigned to wearing that cape for a little while longer. Are you happy about this? If you are honest, the answer is probably NO. We do NOT want to control everything, it is unfair and exhausting, but this level of uncertainty is scary for us and our children so we step up instead. The question is, why are men behaving in this way? Why do they not opt for option 3 as a matter of natural evolution? Maybe, just maybe, they are feeling vulnerable and unsure as in our quest for equality, we have blasted them when they have! Because we have said, 'I don't need a man, I am perfectly capable of looking after myself, I am not weak, I do not do vulnerable, blah blah!'

We have become so capable, smart, savvy and inde-pendent that we appear not to need men anymore. We also live in a society where violence and abuse towards women is increasing and seen as an acceptable norm (I will discuss this later), so our reluctance to embrace our vulnerability is understandable. However, there are lots of good men out there too, but they are getting the message that we do not need them and this is chipping away at their masculinity just as Superwoman, over time, erodes our glorious, graceful, gentle femininity.

We may have done all of this for the right reasons but it only serves to keep us stuck in the exhausting Super-woman model. Until we let go, men will not step up and we will be left holding all the cards, managing our own certainty and feeling powerless in a model that we created to make us feel in control!

How do I get my certainty? I know without any doubt that Tony will protect me, look after me, if necessary stand in front of a moving train or a dragon to save me, and it empowers me to let go. I also know that if he was not around I am more than capable of looking after myself. I did before I met him and if I ever find myself without him I will again. But I see little point in competing for his energy when I am with him, as he does this far better than me and loves it. It is part of his identity as a man and I am secure enough in myself and in him to let go and place my trust in him. This gives me certainty whilst simultaneously hitting all his buttons too.

Let's be clear before we move on: I have no certainty that he will wash up to my standards, no certainty that if I ask him to bring back buttermilk from the supermarket he will find it, no certainty that he will remember we are going to a wedding a week on Saturday, certainly no certainty that he even cares about who or what is in fashion this month. But I have complete certainty that he will stand up for me in a fight, put me first at the sight or smell of danger, do what is necessary to ensure I feel safe, secure and loved, and be vigilant protecting our environment and our liberty. That's certainty. It's about the big stuff, NOT the detail.

Cherished/Loved

We both need to feel loved but the way this love is demonstrated is quite different between the sexes. He feels love when we are suitably impressed by his valour or wisdom, he feels loved when we praise his achievements or trust his judgment. Although we may appreciate recognition for any of the above it is not what we need to feel truly loved. We need to be cherished. It's all about the little stuff for us, the detail, the actions that show he cares and he has thought about us, about what we like, what will make us laugh, what we need, now. It is the post-it note on the fridge, the flowers for no reason, holding our hand, stealing a kiss when we are engaged in some mundane activity, surprising us with an act of kindness. All these little things sing love to us. They make us feel that we matter, that love is eternal, that we are still present in his thoughts. We need that validation, he generally does not. Another term for this could be romance, although when I think about the things my husband does for me that make me feel cherished some of them would never be termed romantic in the traditional sense!

I know for sure Tony cherishes me. I know from the things he does that I am in his thoughts many times in his day. I don't expect to be there all the time, far be it from me to distract him from earning my admiration! But I know he cares and understands me and in the same way that I meet his needs consciously and in many cases unconsciously through my behaviour and body language he does the same for me.

- He will light a fire if he senses I am getting chilly.
- If we travel together he always drives so I can make calls and enjoy the ride.

- He will pop his head into the library where I write and work after a few hours to see if I need anything.
- He will see to the car when he knows I am taking a trip further than the local village. He will check oil, water, tyres etc and even fill the car with petrol as he knows I hate doing this.
- He always holds my hand when out walking ANYWHERE and has to walk on the outside, nearest the road.
- He takes control of our travel arrangements as he knows I am a ditzy adventurer (it's part of my charm) and not the world's most confident flyer.
- He sends me texts telling me he misses me, is proud of me and loves me when I am out and he knows I am in a tough meeting.
- He nurtures my girlie spirit. He loves my feminine side. He is fascinated by my take on life, my opinions, my compassion and my unwavering, emotional connection to everything!

Do I need to go on? Are you cursing him yet? Are you jealous? Do you think he is a mirage and not real? Do you think he is playing me and not genuine? Are you kidding yourself that you do not want this anyway – it would make you feel uncomfortable, weak, suffocated or sabotage your hard-won independence? Or are you resigned to the fact that he is one of a kind and men like this do not exist anymore? Do you want to know if he has a brother?

I have heard it all. But remember Superwoman will never find Superman. They are both fictional characters. A real relationship is one where energies are aligned. It is a well-oiled machine, a perfect team, where both players are happy and grounded in their natural space. All this happens without too much effort when it is right. In fact, it has taken some effort for Tony and I to actually define why and how our relationship works as we behave in this way unconsciously!

A key part of being cherished is being complimented.

Complimented

We need to hear appreciation. Men are more than happy to accept the odd compliment too every now and again, but their external validation is driven far more by actions than words.

Imagine the scenario....

the black or silver shoes, darling?

You and your love are off out to a glamorous charity ball. He is suited and booted on time and enjoying a swift malt whisky as he loiters downstairs awaiting your entrance. You on the other hand are trapped in a dilemma – which shoes...? You take a deep breath and saunter downstairs and proclaim 'Ta dah! I am wearing this dress!' to which he nods and says 'OK, let's go, we are going to be late.' But you do not move. Now you display both pairs of shoes, look him right in the eye and say, 'So, darling, I can't decide which shoes go best. What do you think? Black sexy stilettos or strappy silver mules?' The question every red-blooded male dreads! It hangs in the air for rather too long as he shifts from foot to foot feeling the onset of panic, recognizing that he is trapped. He knows each choice will result in a defensive reply from you asking what is wrong with the others, if he says both you will take it as disinterest, if he says you know best he will also get rebuffed. What to do? But let's take a barefooted step back a moment.

Are you seriously interested in his opinion on your foot-wear? Remember, this is the man who is colour blind, has no interest in fashion, clothes or style and would not recognize a designer label if his life depended on it! Be honest, is that really why you paraded in front of him when you were almost ready to leave? Don't we do this when we are feeling unloved, uncherished and in need of a compliment? Don't we just want to know that we look beautiful? That we still make him smile? That we still rock his world? You see, if we have reached the point when we are asking ridiculous, irrelevant questions about our clothes choice, colour choice etc, we are already feeling neglected. Tony knows that if I have to ask he has already missed the boat. If I pose questions on my appearance, taste or style I am simply in need of some validation that he has failed to read.

Again, this is a question of detail and not feeling like we are being taken for granted. It matters to us and we often go all around the houses attempting to get it!

And finally, the topic of conversation amongst women everywhere when they get together to moan about their men – COMMUNICATION. Why won't he talk to me? He never tells me how he feels, he just does not listen to me, I am fed up repeating everything and screaming to be heard!

Communication

First of all let's get real and accept that women are simply better communicators than men. We listen and hear more, are open, get into rapport fast, think and process information simultaneously. Watching a group of women in conversation is like watching a perfectly rehearsed, multifaceted, intricate dance sequence. We use all our senses, we read each other's body language, we all talk at the same time but can still follow the thread of the conversation and we are so connected we can even finish each other's sentences or move onto to another topic without even bothering to complete the last one because we are all on the same page! A gesture can replace several sentences, we can talk, eat, observe and shop at the same time and we possess a high social dynamic that allows many of us to problem solve through the medium of conversation. In short, we need to talk.

give me your soul or nothing, thanks....

But oh, if talking was all we needed! Most of us have to have an emotional connection. Observing women at business networks over the years has highlighted this need very clearly to me. Men work the room, handing out business cards, selling themselves and their services with ease. Within a two-hour meeting they can speak to well over 40% of the delegates and leave feeling satisfied that they have done the business. Women, on the other hand will have connected with less than 20% of the room, often only one or two people, but the dialogue will have been more in depth, more personal and more expansive. Women need relationships, men need transactions. We build relationships, men collect contacts. There are benefits to both approaches from a purely entrepreneurial perspective but intimacy to a woman is impossible without deep, emotional connection and this is about sharing everything from your hopes, fears, dreams and feelings to your favourite colour and pizza of choice!

If we are denied access to our man's soul we rebel. This can take the form of sulking, physical withdrawal, nagging, creating arguments to get a reaction, unreasonable demands on his time and resources, to name a few. Communication is not just a 'nice to have' it is a fundamental need and without it we wilt or get angry. The beautiful and inspiring poem *The Invitation* from the book of the same name by Oriah Mountain Dreamer sums this up perfectly for me:

It doesn't interest me
what you do for a living.
I want to know
what you ache for
and if you dare to dream
of meeting your heart's longing.

It doesn't interest me
how old you are.
I want to know
if you will risk
looking like a fool
for love
for your dream
for the adventure of being alive.

It doesn't interest me
what planets are
squaring your moon...
I want to know
if you have touched
the centre of your own sorrow
if you have been opened
by life's betrayals
or have become shriveled and closed
from fear of further pain.

I want to know
if you can sit with pain
mine or your own
without moving to hide it

or fade it
or fix it.

I want to know
if you can be with joy
mine or your own
if you can dance with wildness
and let the ecstasy fill you
to the tips of your fingers and toes
without cautioning us to be careful
to be realistic
to remember the limitations
of being human.

It doesn't interest me
if the story you are telling me
is true.
I want to know if you can
disappoint another
to be true to yourself.
If you can bear
the accusation of betrayal
and not betray your own soul.
If you can be faithless
and therefore trustworthy.

I want to know if you can see Beauty
even when it is not pretty
every day.
And if you can source your own life
from its presence.

I want to know
if you can live with failure
yours and mine
and still stand at the edge of the lake
and shout to the silver of the full moon,
"Yes."

It doesn't interest me
to know where you live
or how much money you have.
I want to know if you can get up
after the night of grief and despair
weary and bruised to the bone
and do what needs to be done
to feed the children.

It doesn't interest me
who you know
or how you came to be here.
I want to know if you will stand
in the centre of the fire
with me
and not shrink back.

It doesn't interest me
where or what or with whom
you have studied.
I want to know
what sustains you
from the inside
when all else falls away.

I want to know
if you can be alone
with yourself
and if you truly like
the company you keep
in the empty moments.

My husband always quotes a line from one of Allan and Barbara Pease's many books on the differences between the sexes. Apparently, according to them, women use over 14,000 words a day as opposed to men, who only use 7,000. I have no idea how true this is but it seems pretty obvious to me that most women talk more than men. Tony tells me that on an average day a fully employed guy will use most of his 7,000 words at work so that by the time he gets home he is more than content to kick back and 'fire gaze' (watch TV). Often at that point, however, we women have not even started and still have at least another two to three thousand left to disseminate so whether they like it or not our men are going to get them, unless our mother or best friend calls or a night out is planned, then they are off the hook!

Again, I am not totally sold on this concept as I know many men that can out-talk me any day, but I am happy to subscribe to some of it, if it means I can get my needs met!

This need to engage in meaningful, mutually bonding, intimate conversations is compromised when we play the Superwoman card as we, in effect, silence men with our controls and demands. When we become their mothers they act out as children – why wouldn't they? The more we nag, the more they rebel. We need to understand their needs too: remember acknowledge, appreciate and admire? If we continually tell them what to do and how to do it, cracks will appear.

Here is a useful exercise to try today to check your Superwoman status: ask your husband/partner/other half to do something for you – but resist the tendency to also tell him how to do it! If you are telling him how to do it you are too controlling. Being aware of this creates a powerful shift in your relationship as you stop trying to control the whole show. I am generally pretty well grounded in my female space, however, when I am stressed I can often revert to Superwoman and it never gets me what I want as my husband does not react well to this behaviour model and we end up falling out. Here is a recent example…

helping or taking over – you decide…

I was due to speak at a conference in Kent. Tony had accompanied me because we were attending an event in London together on the same evening and had not made a decision about whether to stay in London overnight. We arrived in Kent, parked up in the shopping centre and made our way to the venue. We were discussing our best travel options for later and agreed to leave the car in Kent and get the train into the city after my engagement. I asked Tony to sort this out whilst I was speaking but I got a little carried away with my request. It went like this:

'So, babe, whilst I am speaking can you sort out the arrangements for later? If we park here and get the train into London, you need to make sure we are parked in a 24-hour car park so we don't get locked in, if it closes before 10pm better to move it. You can go to the tourist information office in the mall and ask where the nearest 24-hour car park is. Then contact the event organiser at the London venue and find out what time the seminar we are going to finishes and then work out if we can get back to Kent at a reasonable time to make the journey back home tonight, otherwise find out how much is a room for the night, and if it's crazy have a look at the surrounding hotels. Oh and also don't forget to factor in the cost of the 24-hour car park.'

As I am sure you can imagine Tony was getting more and more frustrated with me and eventually he lost it and said, 'For God's sake Jane, I am not a 5 year old. I am perfectly capable of sorting this out on my own. I don't need step-by-step instructions, just leave it with me. Good luck with your gig!' then he stormed off and I was left feeling upset and not in the best of states to inspire an audience of over 400 female entrepreneurs! Fortunately, I am a professional and know how to control my state so I did my stuff and had a chance to reflect on the conversation that got Tony so frustrated.

I asked for his help, I communicated. I asked him to solve a problem, to fix something. This is all I needed to do for him to step up and do his stuff, but I then proceeded to patronize him and tell him how to do it too! You see, I thought I was helping him, fast tracking the information for him but he saw me trying to control him, assuming he was incapable of looking after me and that is the worst thing I could have intimated. Don't we do this too often? I still have to keep this one in check. So try it, stop after you have asked the question: 'So babe, whilst I am speaking can you sort out the arrangements for later?'

no-one is perfect...

I am not advocating the perfect relationship here, there's no such thing: the key is learning and growing together and accepting that sometimes we get it wrong but our heart is in the right place! I slip into my Superwoman cape when I am stressed and sometimes Tony lets me wear it and sometimes he gently reminds me I have it on! He sometimes tries to fix me when all I want is to rant and sometimes I let him and sometimes I ask for silence.

So, to summarise, we need to feel cherished and appreciated. We need touch, compliments, romance and every now and again a bit of spontaneity. We need to feel connected on an emotional level, which we develop through regular communication, and we need to be heard. However, all of this is a non-starter without certainty.

Superwoman will sabotage our needs by taking over certainty and controlling a one-way communication channel: you to him, you to him, you to him. Wearing the cape and badge that screams absolute self-sufficiency will exclude him, marginalize his input and make him feel disconnected and discontinued!

is this the real world as we know it?

I know for many of you this sounds like a dream. A self-assured man, ready to step up and look after his woman and family, a protector and provider (remember, this is not about money) in touch with his female side, emotionally connected to you and his kids. A strong, powerful and focused man that gives you absolute certainty, thus in turn allowing you to let go, to give up your Superwoman cape and embrace your authentic, feminine core.

As Laura Doyle states in her book *The Surrendered Wife*:

> *'Why be a chauffeur when you can be the VIP? When you give up unnecessary control of the things your part-ner does – how he drives, what he wears, what he does at work, how he loads the dishwasher etc – you actually*

gain power in the relationship and in your life. Doing all the work is not what makes you powerful. On the other hand, relaxing and enjoying yourself while someone else takes care of things is a very powerful position to be in. Certainly the VIP who rides in the limousine is more powerful than the chauffeur who controls the vehicle.'

I know hundreds of women that have this level of intimacy and understanding in their relationship, they just do not feel the need to shout about it.

top ten relationship rants when superwoman is present

from her to him...

1. Stop fixing me – just listen, support and care.

2. When I want your advice I will ask, until I do just make oohhh and aahhh noises, thank you.

3. Step up and do something around here, why wait to be asked? We live in the same house, you can see what I see and despite the urban myths clothes do not jump into the washer unaided, nor does the fridge automatically restock and yes I do know the gas bill is due.

4. What happened to romance? You never tell me I am beautiful, act spontaneously, sweep me off my feet, make small gestures that show you still

care, and NO, petrol station carnations once in a blue moon do NOT count.

5. Take control for God's sake! I am fed up making all the decisions around here. I organize everything – the home, our leisure time, the bills, our holidays, keeping up with friends and family. Are you sure you can speak and count?

6. Why is it all down to me? I am exhausted, I need to be looked after once in a while, I feel alone, my knight in shining armour has deserted me – oh look, he is on the golf course again!

and from him to her...

1. Stop nagging and telling me what to do – you are not my mother. I need space to make my own decisions, you are silencing me and making me feel disrespected and untrustworthy by constantly telling me what to do – get some duct tape!

2. You are too high maintenance – I have no idea what you want, you change your mind all the time and whatever I do I get it wrong or it is never to your standards.

3. I am redundant around here, we are supposed to be a team, but I have no say, no control and no respect.

4. I am fed up having to mind read. Just tell me
   what you want, not how to get it! Be specific,
   ask, be direct – don't ask via a question, express your desire. I want to make you happy,
   I am more than capable of finding the solution,
   just tell me, please.

I am pretty sure you could add some more to this list,
and I am also pretty sure that if you are polishing your
Superwoman badge as you read this you will now be
feeling very disorientated and pretty mad about the
whole area of CONTROL. You see, you think I am telling
you that you are not entitled to control. It is a man's
game and you need to get back in your 'little woman
box' and learn to shut up, be nice, stay small and flutter
your eyelashes more. I get that you are annoyed and
want to give me a lecture on liberation and the fight for
independence. I get that this is uncomfortable and I feel
your anger. However, I believe female energy is power.
I believe being a woman is more than enough and our
authenticity, however controversial, is worth fighting for
so I salute you for engaging in the debate with me and
let's continue our journey by discussing the heart of
male energy – CONTROL...

men need control – oh, do they indeed!

If you are controlling everything, you have in fact shifted
the energy in your relationship and you are now firmly in
his territory. Men exert power through control, women

exert power through attraction. This is the crux of the matter, so let's spend some time illuminating this.

Men are egocentric, they need to feel in control of themselves and, to a degree, their surroundings to feel whole. This control is what attracts us in the first place! We like a man that is confident, self-assured and driven. We are programmed to seek the hunter/gatherer, provider and protector model and he needs to be well grounded in his male energy to project this. But if we then go on to play our Superwoman game, not allowing him any control, conflict is inevitable. Now let's be clear, I said control, NOT controlling. His role is not about controlling you, it is about control over himself and his life. Big difference. I am not for one minute condoning violence, coercion or manipulation, in fact, this is the total opposite. A man that has these characteristics is totally out of control.

Male energy is aggressive with a fight mentality. If you threaten him or his family, a man in his male energy will react. In the middle of the night a sound outside causes concern and suspicion – who jumps out of bed to check it out? Who's on guard? Who's ready to fight to protect? If you are honest with yourself you hope, pray and even expect it to be him. This reaction is often sexy in him but a little intimidating and ugly when you do it from your male energy. We are supposed to behave differently. Same problem, different reaction. Just think about global conflict and wars. If we had more women in positions of power and influence in government and politics do you think we would have more or less military action? Female energy is grounded in peace, harmony and collaboration. We are uncomfortable with aggression, our response is more passive, we are more likely to say, 'Let's talk about it, let's find a non-violent, win/win resolution.'

The key is that male and female energy are supposed to co-exist in perfect harmony when balanced. In other words, they need us and we need them. We are a well-oiled team, but only when our energy is aligned. It's a Yin/Yang thing!

This works in my house. I cannot tell you how many times I have talked my husband out of choosing an unnecessarily aggressive response to a situation and after I have calmed him down he says, 'You were so right about that Jane, I over-reacted,' or 'I was just letting off steam.'

It also works the other way, he encourages me to step up and use my male energy in many situations, saying 'Jane, you need to assert yourself here, you are being taken advantage of,' or 'You are too soft.' He is usually right!

If we are honest with ourselves, the very things we crave in a man, we also despair of and foolishly try to change! The Alpha male is making a comeback, Mr Metrosexual is under threat. I accept my views may not be universal but most women I speak to want a strong, powerful no-nonsense, real man. When you consider the pin ups of the modern, 35+ women the following hunks appear on the list every time: Russell Crowe (only in The Gladiator for me, but it's more than enough), Mr Big, the archetypal Alpha male from the Sex And The City movies, Jason Statham, Bruce Willis, Samuel L. Jackson, Clive Owen, Colin Farrell, Daniel Craig.

You do not have to agree with my list, and I am sure you could add a few more, but there is no denying all these men are grounded in their male energy – egos are on full alert, they are aggressive, focused, driven, competitive and ambitious. Without having personal relationships with any of them (damn, on the Russell Crowe front!), just from their public behaviour – and, in the case of the movie stars, the roles they choose – it is not difficult to observe their energy and the effect this has on women.

When I ask women, 'Why these men, how do they make you feel?', in between the odd 'Pwhoar!' and drooling, all of them talk about these men making them feel safe, protected, like a woman, feminine, frustrated some-times but you know where you are with them. They are powerful and this is sexy and very attractive.

What they are describing is CONTROL. It is hard to deny our attraction to powerful men, history is littered with examples, as are the tabloids and the movies. But what we are also seeing is the emergence of the Alpha female too and this throws us into confusion again. My question to you is this….

Consider the Alpha female, think Angelina Jolie, Katie Price (aka Jordan), Madonna. These woman are operating far more from their male energy – they behave like men, are low on emotions, controlling, competitive, tough, with few female friends, egocentric, action orientated with hard bodies and even harder exteriors. There is no denying they are successful, but at what price? You decide: is the Alpha female (or beta male as she is sometimes called) a derogatory label created by men or a complimentary label created by women? Is this the future or a happy place for the minority? By the way men have several unpleasant and often offensive names for women embracing this identity and I am sure I don't need to repeat any of them here.

vulnerability is power to real women

My husband and I have worked with many couples via relationship coaching and have also run workshops on male/female energy so to balance this debate, here is what we get from men of a certain age whenever we ask them to share their pin ups and the reasons why...

Nigella Lawson, Susan Sarandon, Meryl Streep, Jennifer Aniston, Marilyn Monroe (still), Beyoncé, Helen Mirren. They describe these women as passionate, bright, intelligent, intuitive, self-assured, soft, feminine, and feisty with hidden depth and strength. When we ask them the same question, 'How do they make you feel?' they say, 'I want to look after them, protect them, I want them to be as proud of me as I would be proud of them. They have a certain sparkle yet I know they would not overpower me, they are successful without the need to be ruthless and I just know they are vulnerable in certain areas of their life and I like that.'

Now listen up ladies, one word that is never uttered in describing these women is WEAK. They talk about vulnerability as a positive trait, NOT a weakness. That is our baggage. Who told us being honest, open and real was wrong? When did we stop being authentic? What is clever about pretending everything is OK and believing it is weak to show any vulnerability at any time? Intimacy and emotional connection demand openness and honesty. I understand many of us have been hurt, been in relationships with men who have abused our vulnerability and we have had to get tough to survive, but until we open our hearts true love will elude us and we will continue to attract the wrong men: men happy to let us do everything, men who are so insecure in themselves that they are happy to ride on our success for as long as we let them, men who are lost and attempt to create their personal security by controlling us instead of themselves, men whose warped response to losing control is violence, and many more no-hopers.

Your vulnerability is your core. It is you being true to you, and it is precious. Real men need and deserve this part of you more than ever. This is what allows them to step up and embrace their masculine spirit. It is like you giving them permission to be male. Hiding it from them only highlights your insecurities. If you love you, you are proud that this love is all-embracing. You celebrate your foibles as well as your talents. It is all part of your greatness and THAT is power. A woman who is at peace with who she is, her values, her needs, her dreams, her talents, her vulnerabilities – that is a woman that lights up a room, shines and is like a drug for real men!

I am a strong, sassy, successful woman, who runs several businesses, speaks internationally, lives with passion with a big vision and is surrounded by amazing people and opportunities. I am also not afraid to show my vulnerability. I get it wrong sometimes, I feel fear, I feel overwhelmed and anxious, I cry, I stress over the little stuff, I often take on too much, etc, etc. But the only person that truly knows my emotional state at all times is my husband. You see I give him my vulnerability as a gift and he steps up and protects that gift with his life. Because I open my heart and soul to him he is in no doubt about my intentions towards him and in return I get the emotional connection, love and the absolute devotion I crave. Bingo! Jackpot! Cha ching! You see, men need somewhere safe to store their vulnerabilities too, and that is YOU!

'I am selfish, impatient and a little insecure. I make mistakes, I am out of control and at times hard to handle.

But if you cannot handle me at my worst, then you sure as hell don't deserve me at my best.'

Marilyn Monroe

Vulnerability is power. It is your secret weapon, it is your love and it is worth fighting for. It allows you to be real, authentic and celebrate your true feminine self, no need to hide or pretend. This is who you are and you are amazing!

It goes without saying that if your gift is rejected or abused, the game is over. He blew it, he does not deserve you, trust is history and so is he.

the alpha female - here to stay or fad?

Men in their male energy are generally NOT attracted to women in their male energy and vice versa. How many of us, honestly, feel connected to guys that sit in their female energy? Please do not misinterpret my premise here: I demand emotional connection with my soul mate, I want access to his feminine side, but I don't want him to live there permanently. We are talking genetics here, when men and women are in a relationship where they are both in their male energy conflict is not far away. Competition ensues with a constant fight for control and low emotional connection. However, relationships can and do change over time. Sometimes for the better, sometimes not. Take a look around you, what do you see?

I know that for many women the strong woman and vulnerability debate is uncomfortable to comprehend and/or accept, and you are probably cursing me and this book already, but your curiosity is engaged and this is the only thing keeping you in. I will take that and thank you for staying sticky and ask you to remember this: after confusion comes clarity and maybe, just maybe, you are here for a reason and it is time for you to reflect on some of this stuff. If your relationships at work and home are bliss and you are fulfilled, loved, respected and excited about life, my intuition tells me this book would not be in front of you now.

Eve Ensler, author, playwright, performer and leading activist campaigning to stop violence against women and girls, refers to this as 'destroying the girl cell'. In her latest work *I am an Emotional Creature: The secret life of girls around the world* she discusses how the girl cell is being systematically destroyed, suppressed and eradicated from our society. We are told to get tough, harden up, stop crying, stop feeling, don't take it personally! We are conditioned to believe that all our female values – emotions, vulnerability, compassion, passion, empathy, openness, intuition, intensity and nurturing – are weaknesses.

We bring up the world NOT to be a girl.

To be a boy is NOT to be a girl.

To be a man is NOT to be a girl.

To be a woman is NOT to be a girl.

To be a leader is NOT to be a girl.

To be strong is NOT to be a girl.

In fact Ensler believes that being a GIRL is so powerful, we have all been trained NOT to be one!

I ask you to open your heart and mind to the possibility that we may be buying into some powerful, negative messages that in turn, are deconstructing our identities as women.

letting go of superwife

Remember, a Diva is a woman who knows who she is and loves herself. She knows what is important to her and what she wants. She embraces her female energy, lives with balance, love, passion and authenticity and is a role model to other women and young girls. She knows her greatness and shines.

It is not what you say that matters, it is what you do. Change your behaviour not your rants/nags. Let his discovery be your action, NOT your words. The key is to show as opposed to tell! Be aware that if you have been playing the Superwoman game for a long time, and maybe attracted him whilst in it, behaviour patterns will not shift overnight. He needs to see you are serious about change. Consistency is the key.

Give him back some control but do it with love, not accusation. None of the following statements will help the cause or have the desired effect:

> *'Right, apparently I have got to trust you and listen to you and let you make some decisions – God help us!!'*

> *'OK, I am not supposed to give you advice or tell you what to do, according to this book you are more than capable of deciding for yourself, even though I know you are not.'*

> *'I am going to trust you from now on, makes you feel like a man I am told.'*

> *'I am going to pretend I trust you, even though I don't. We are going to play the fake-it-til-you-make-it game, OK?'*

Embrace your vulnerability. Take tiny steps. Let go of some small stuff and see what happens. Be open with your feelings, don't be afraid to cry, ask for help when you need it and be specific about what you need.

Stop blaming and start trusting. Tell him what you want and need then let him deliver, and try not to criticise his approach.

Give up on perfection. Be real, accept that the lessons and learnings are in the moments of failure. Own your mistakes and let him own his. Get used to living with a bit of chaos. Life is too short to spend all your joint leisure time cleaning!

Watch your language and stop telling him what to do. Let him rise to the challenges his own way. If the outcome is the same and the problem gets solved, who cares how?

Nurture your feminine spirit – get precious about your 'me time'. All work and no play is not healthy and leads to resentment, guilt and exhaustion. Spend time with your girlfriends, they help you get perspective and understand your worth.

Embrace your inner girl. Stop apologising for being emotional, compassionate and soft. Re-engage with your playful side, stop taking yourself so seriously and have some fun.

Enjoy being cherished – give him permission to love you and take care of you.

Tune into his needs – make him feel loved and admired and remember to say thank you, he doesn't want to be taken for granted either.

'Superwife got me seeking 'physical perfection' and so I was starved for most of my twenties, size 8 (not a good look for me) and exhausted and close to tears most of the time – not a lot of fun to be around...

The solution was for me to spend time getting to know and understand me and the need for honest and open communication, firstly with myself and then everyone else, plus regain a sense of humour (I had been a funny kid)! Also ditch the man and go and surround myself with more meaningful work and relationships. Today, I try and live my life by my mantra: 'Be interested and interesting...'

Laurel, a Diva, married, an adventurer and an IT professional

I listen to so many tales of woe from single women today about the lack of good men, the desperate dating scene and the stress of never finding Mr Right. When I intimate that this may have something to do with their attraction strategy, Superwoman stands tall, takes a deep breath and regales me with all the reasons why this is nothing to do with her:

> *'I am a smart woman, independent and a catch – most men are just looking for a bimbo who doesn't answer back and that's not me...'*

> *'I don't need a man anyway, but I would like a little fun, on my terms, every now and again...'*

'The older I get, the more choosy I become and now I am unwilling to compromise. I have worked hard for what I have got and I am not throwing it away on just anyone. He will have to be pretty special to get in my knickers...'

'I like the idea of living separate lives and just having intimacy on my terms, you know like spending the odd weekend together or 2/3 nights a week but I have a busy life, great girlfriends and a high-pressure job so I can't just drop all that anytime soon...'

'Most men are just looking for a mother figure, they are incapable of handling a career woman like me...'

'I am not interested in getting married again. I am looking for a self- sufficient guy, wealthy and charming who will wine and dine me, treat me like a princess and not expect complete devotion in return. I am looking for no-strings-attached fun, but if it turns into something more I may reconsider...'

'He has got to be tall, slim, with his own hair and teeth, financially comfortable with his own house and a degree of emotional intelligence. I have kissed enough frogs...'

'I have decided not to have any relationships with men until my children are older. I feel it is unfair to expect them to connect with another man other than their father so I will just keep it casual and under the radar...'

Unfortunately, these are all genuine comments I have been privy to over the years from sassy, attractive, smart, successful women. Do you see any patterns here? Are you surprised they are eternally single? Can you make an educated guess at the kind of men they attract?

Single Superwoman is a tough cookie on the dating scene. She tends to control who, what, where, how and how often. Undoubtedly, some men will like this but a man grounded in his male energy, the one most of them really want and need, will walk on by. Regardless of how physically attractive and charming they appear, the prospect is simply too daunting, too much like hard work, too high maintenance, too competitive and too combative.

Some men may perceive Superwoman as a challenge and manage to break through the 'ice queen' act and you may live happily ever after, but – forgive me for daring to suggest – there is an easier way that expands your options as opposed to playing this pretty high-risk strategy.

The majority of comments here are defensive and come from a fear of disappointment. There is an unwillingness to let go, to surrender to the process, be open and dare I say vulnerable (are we OK with that word now?). Placing such high expectations on this 'ideal man' is a sure-fire way of never finding him and that is fine too because then you can never get hurt. Attempting to control what is a spontaneous and often random happening – love – is a recipe for self-sabotage. Superwoman professes to have all these demands to keep her safe. Control is the fall-back position and the inability to commit is denial.

Whilst I recognise an element of self-preservation is necessary to enter the dating environment, Superwoman is intimidating, a turn-off and an altogether terrifying prospect for most guys.

How many times have you heard your girlfriends attempt to play matchmaker? Superwomen position the opportunity like this: 'Well, Jane is a real catch. She is intelligent, dynamic and a real powerhouse. She is a high flyer with the salary to match, does not suffer fools, drives a sports car, lives in an amazing house, is well travelled, well read and enjoys the best life can offer. Any man should consider themselves very lucky to have the opportunity to take her out.'

Now, personally, Jane sounds amazing and I would date her! But most red-blooded males may feel a tad insecure at the prospect. Our idea of what constitutes a catch and theirs are very different. I am not suggesting that men want shy, dumb airheads! It is all in the positioning. Every Superwoman has a heart of gold, a soft, feminine, girlie side, passion, emotional intelligence, charm and wit, but this tends to be hidden behind the tough, controlling exterior and this is NOT a turn-on and will not create attraction.

Most men are looking for a woman to share their life, not a competitive partner to spar with. They already have this with their mates and work colleagues. They will relish the challenge once they are in love with you but may not necessarily step up to the plate for this on day one!

What follows are my suggestions for letting go, shifting your behaviour and surrendering to the attraction process. You cannot control everything, you can only put yourself in the best possible position to play and have fun along the way.

ditch the single badge

Many women wear the single badge with pride. It becomes such an ingrained part of their identity that they struggle to rip it off regardless of the love opportunities around them. They use the term to define themselves: 'Hi, I'm Jane. I'm 42, **single** and an entrepreneur.' As you continue to do this everywhere you go, to everyone you meet, the term 'single' takes on a life of its own, it gets recognised, validated and esteemed. It appears over-important to you and something you want to keep. Bottom-line, it keeps you single!

You start to behave like a single person and speak like a single person. You create a life only suitable for a single person, you are attracted to other single people who love being single. The single bit of your identity gets far too much headspace and starts to make the rules. Does this make sense?

You become the confident, fun and storytelling single girl that entertains all your other friends, particularly the few who are attached, with dating horror stories, adventures and hilarious mishaps. They positively look forward to the next instalment of your single life and tell all their friends about you.

You share these short stories on Facebook and Twitter and even have your own blog! You become known for your single status and other singles ask for your advice. In fact, they are in awe of your complete ease and confidence in your singledom.

You develop plans both short and long term to support and consolidate your single status. You convince yourself that some people are just meant to be single and you are happy with this because to admit to anything else would be treason. When another woman expresses the view that being single is just a temporary state you go into overdrive presenting the case for the defence: 'Single is a way of life, it is not temporary, we don't all have to be loved up, there is not someone for everyone, monogamy is a lie and the concept of a soul mate is just an over-inflated fairy tale!' You preach this to all who dare to ask if you are still single, as if they don't already know, and are quick to dismiss the notion of love at first sight or love at all!

Single becomes your friend, your ticket, your comforter. If I asked you to list all the benefits of staying single versus falling in love or being part of a loving couple your response would, predictably, position singledom as the Holy Grail.

The longer you stay attached to this identity, the longer you stay single. It becomes a self-fulfilling prophecy. Single is what single does. When you show up at the wine bar for a night out with your single girlfriends, or even when you are doing your weekly shop at the supermarket, this single badge is like an aroma: it arrives before you do. It is very easy to spot and can act as a red flag for many men as a woman so in love with her single status is likely to give him a hard time, be fun but not for keeps, make a fool out of him, keep him at a distance or hurt him. These messages are so contradictory are they not? Because the main reason for being so precious about this single badge in the first place was to avoid being hurt!

Please do not misinterpret my musings here, I get that there is a time to be single, and jumping from one relationship to another with no breathing space in between is not ideal. We all need space to heal, reconnect with ourselves and simply enjoy our own company every now and again, but I hope I am making it clear that I am not referring to this nourishing, liberating stage of singledom here.

When being single becomes a way of life, ingrained in your identity, who you are, you will pro-actively arrange everything in your environment to retain the status quo. As Anthony Robbins says, 'The strongest force in human nature is the need to remain consistent in how we define ourselves.'

If you are fed up of being single and ready to step up to even just the possibility of love, this badge needs to go.

opening our hearts

Until we acknowledge our desire for love, we will not manifest it in our lives. I know this may sound a bit 'New Age', but as every personal development advocate will tell you – you get what you focus on. If you focus on single you get more single; if you focus on sharing your life with your Mr Right and your desire for love, guess what...?

As this single label has become more like your manifesto than a status description, you now need to change the behaviours, language and thought processes that are keeping you addicted to singledom.

Here are some ideas for a new manifesto – the ready, open and positively-batting-them-off plan!

stop looking and start attracting

Most Superwomen see dating as a project. One they want to control from beginning to end, with targets, milestones, specific criteria, performance monitoring, ranking and a regular review process. They engage in this project on an ad hoc basis, because, as it very rarely works, they become disillusioned and ditch it, until being single gets lonely again or they have other needs to satisfy and the plan, or a new plan with the same strategy, comes back out again…

> *'I have had enough of this dating thing for a while, I will give it another go after Christmas, for now I am concentrating my efforts on work and my daughter!'*

I know if I say this does not work someone will write to me telling me how they met their husband perfectly well doing this, so I am not going to say never, I am just going to ask, 'Is it working for you?' If so, continue; but if it is time for a new plan, listen up…

sexy is what sexy does…

Men are attracted to confident, self-assured women who know who they are, what they want and what is important to them. Women who are comfortable in their own skin, who allow a sliver of light to shine on their vulnerability, giving him a sign, an opening, a chance to have a place in their life. This is sex appeal in action. Sexy is a way of being. You cannot buy it online, copy it or turn it on and off like a light switch. It is you in your authentic state. It is not about how you look, what you wear, the colour of your hair, dress size or pout. It is the whole package. We all know women that do not fit the media's version of beautiful that are serious man magnets! They walk into a bar and the energy around them glows, men are intrigued and interested and powerless to resist. We have watched in awe as these women, with very little effort, create a buzz of male attention. They shine.

When you try too hard to be sexy with the clothes you wear, flesh you bare and exaggerated signalling, the messages are often misinterpreted and you come across as a sexual predator, not a good strategy for attracting Mr Right but perfect for Mr Right Now, for one night only.

Sexy radiates a glow. It is like energy, if it could talk, this is what it would say…

- I know I am more than enough, I am not perfect and never want to be.
- I know who I am warts and all and I love me, so I am pretty sure you will too.
- I am all woman, I love my strength and my vulnerability. My responses to life are never predictable, but always real. I go with the flow, sometimes I laugh, sometimes I cry.
- I am emotional, I am compassionate and I need a connection. In return I will love and adore you and promise to protect your heart.
- I love life and I love being a woman – I celebrate my ditziness, my girlie side, my soft, gentle, nurturing soul and make no apologies for who I am.
- I am successful in my own right, I have passion for my work and I am respected. I know my val-

ues and I am secure enough in myself not to compromise them.

- I am an amazing woman, a divine diva, a goddess, a queen, a princess and I am open to love and being cherished and saying hello to my soul mate.

Now, you do not have to agree with everything I have said here, but can you imagine how changed you would be if you genuinely believed and lived every one of those statements? Can you image the energy and vibe you would give off the next time you walked into your local wine bar if you knew all that to be true?

Female is soft and gentle with hidden strength and resolve; it is fun and flirty with an element of mystery; it is kind and welcoming; it is passive and receptive but not weak; it is sensual and playful but not overtly sexual; it is open and intuitive; it is nurturing and caring but no pushover.

Unless you are into nonstandard relationships like S&M, most men are attracted to the combination of sassy and strong with a soft underbelly and this is female energy in flow!

comfortable in your own skin?

Any attempt to appear confident when you are not, ie faking it, is NOT sexy and will not deliver the goods. If you are a great actor, you can pretend all is perfect with your life and be successful at attracting a great guy but when he finds out that you are not 'all that' he may feel cheated and decide to walk.

Confidence comes from knowing who you are and loving you. It stands to reason that if you don't love you, you are hardly going to convince someone else to love you too. But even worse than this, if someone does take the time to see past your insecurities and fall in love with the real you, then you go into panic mode and subconsciously sabotage the situation as follows:

1. You punish him for loving you because you cannot see how or why he loves you, when you don't – you make him jump through hoops continually to prove to you how he feels – how much do you love me? How much do you love me? If you loved me you would do this or that, if you loved me you would not say that, if you loved me you would buy me that, etc.

This is pretty exhausting for the poor guy who loves you, who sees past your tiny flaws, who loves the real you, who can forgive your imperfections and loves all your foibles! Eventually he finds it impossible to watch you destroy yourself, he feels powerless to convince you that you are enough, worthy, amazing – and he leaves.

2. You settle for far less than you deserve because you believe that is all you are worth. You stay in

a relationship that is far past its sell by date for fear that you will not find anyone else.

This is sad, hardly empowering, and a recipe for a very unfulfilling life. The belief that you are not enough will not only compromise your right to love, it will infect every other area of your life. If this has touched a nerve maybe now is the time to do something about it? It may be worth doing some work to uncover your patterns, your script, and your story. How did you get here? And what are you doing to stay in this place? Enrolling on a personal development workshop, doing some more reading, or working with a coach are all options to kick start your personal journey of discovery. It is time you believed in you, that you loved you, unconditionally. Only then will the sexy, sassy diva within come out to play!

Alongside loving yourself, self-assurance and inner confidence come from knowing what is important to you and being absolutely sure about what you will and will not compromise.

discovering your hot buttons

Knowing what is important to you, what you will not compromise on and what you need to feel whole, is for many people the key to unlocking the mystery of self. These are what we call our values. Values are the hot buttons by which we live our lives. They affect our choices, the way we behave, the people we choose to spend time with, our leisure pursuits, the job we do, the business we create and our motivation. These values are stored in our subconscious and work for us without us really being aware of them; like the actions that make our nails grow and our hair longer, they are there and working, but we are not consciously aware of them every day.

However, we do tend to notice them when someone or something attempts to violate them. We feel discomfort, stress, emotional pain, even anger, and if we stay in this place for long enough this starts to affect our self-esteem and confidence big time as we are subconsciously being forced to behave in a way that goes against who we are. The fact that we are allowing this to happen (remember, you own your decisions and choices) just results in us beating ourselves up for our own weaknesses, carrying around more and more guilt, turning this indecision and weak will into self-hate.

The longer we play this game, the more 'out of sorts' we feel. You can walk in someone else's shoes but it is almost impossible to run in them; we become more and more stuck, lose our way, walk towards our goals more slowly, with less spring in our step and lead in our heart.

Just think about the last time you worked in a company where you felt uncomfortable with some elements of the work practices and/or the corporate values. These are often hidden in the unwritten rules and culture of the organisation but in order to survive most people learn them pretty fast! Let's say the firm values commitment in the form of attendance and not outcomes. So the people that get on are the ones whose jackets are on the back of the chairs the longest, not necessarily the employees that achieve the most sales or get through the most work. This happens in many corporates and is a subtle form of discrimination towards working mums, but that is a whole other book!

If your values include honesty and achievement then most days working in this environment are going to chip away at your self-esteem. Even worse, if you are left with no choice but to join them and work later and later just to be seen, you will eventually feel like you are selling your soul in exchange for a pay cheque!

Here's another example. Let's say one of the things you value above all others is creativity – using your imagination, being able to express yourself through your artistic talent – and due, in part, to our education system and lack of guidance you feel unable to feed this value and are encouraged to give it up and join the corporate rat race. How long before you get depressed, feel worthless, feel like you don't fit in, feel on the outside of life, start to turn this in on yourself and translate it into self-hatred?

Or how about this… Your business partner is continually questioning your decisions, he/she always needs more information on anything you propose and quite often will ask the advice of people/suppliers outside the business on options you have put forward before agreeing to anything. They assure you this is nothing to do with you, it is simply their cautious nature and need to gather more information before making decisions. If any of your top values include respect, recognition, status and/or professional credibility, you will feel violated. They, on the other hand, may be operating from a totally different set of values or perhaps their interpretation is not aligned with yours. Either way this situation is not sustainable without having some detrimental effect on your self-esteem.

And finally, on a more personal note, let's say your husband has an affair. Is that a deal breaker for you or not? Can you forgive him? What if he has gambled all your savings? What about if he refuses to mix with your friends or values his solitude over and above spending time with you? Your response to all of these situations will be dependent on the hierarchy of your values. This is why some people can forgive infidelity and others cannot; one person's indiscretion is another's heartbreak and so on. The values on the table here are loyalty, trust, connection, love, intimacy, honesty and tolerance.

uncovering what makes you tick

It is not just the word at play here, such as 'trust' or 'respect', it is our interpretation of that word that is key. Whenever I facilitate sessions on eliciting values either in a group or during a one-to-one coaching session I ask women to think about what is important to them in three key areas of their life:

1. Your intimate relationship – what do you need to be happy and what would be a deal breaker for you? If you are single, what has been a deal breaker in other relationships and why?

2. Your professional life – work or business – what do you need to make it work? To feel you are making a difference?

3. Your home life/family and friends – what is the ideal, what are you striving for? And what would you not accept or put up with?

If you can have a conversation around these three areas your values tend to make themselves known: often this includes a journey into your past to uncover your script, how you have behaved in critical moments, etc.

Once you have clarity on what drives you, the obvious follow-up question is about alignment. How congruent is your life with your values? Is it all in harmony or is there some conflict? If so, where and what can you do about it – because believe me if you do nothing, or have done nothing, the only guarantee is pain. This will show up as low self-esteem, anxiety, guilt, apathy, sadness, stress, depression, addiction and loud, negative internal dialogue as you continue to be self-critical about your lack of resolve to stay true to you.

can we change our values anytime soon?

This is a question only you can answer. Without question our values change over time, as we enter different stages of our life we adjust our needs and wants, but I would dare to suggest that several core values stay the same. For example, if you compare what was driving you in your twenties versus your forties, can you see some shifts? Absolutely: for me my twenties were about recognition, chasing status and money, whereas today I am more driven by love, the need to be authentic, creating financial freedom and contribution. However, if one of your values is loyalty, do you think this would shift with time? Only you can decide to change your values as this demands a shift in your behaviour and environment.

The follow-up question to this is always, 'So what happens if my husband's values are not the same as mine?' Again, this demands some personal soul-searching and sharing with your partner – where are the compromises? Are there any? Where is the conflict? How high up in your hierarchy is the value in question? No two people are exactly alike, your values and your hierarchy and your interpretation is totally unique. Let's say he values adventure and you don't – is this a deal breaker? Probably not, it just means you are likely to have a heated debate on your choice of holiday or the compromise may be that he climbs Kilimanjaro without you! However, what if you valued intimacy and this did not even appear on his top ten? Male and female differences aside, this could be a little more serious.

How much easier would relationship decisions be in terms of dating and commitment if we understood each other's values from day one? Finally we are starting to see the dating industry catch on to this. One of the largest and most successful players is **www.eharmony. com.** They have been operating in the US for over ten years (arrived in the UK in 2009) and claim that in the US 236 eHarmony members marry every day! Their model uses values to assist in the matching process. Their web copy states: 'bringing people together, based on the things that really matter'. Next time you observe a couple that appear to be total opposites, be aware there is so much more going on underneath. This is another reason why it is never a good idea to judge a book by its cover.

So, in order to flaunt our sexy, sassy self we may need to spend a little time reconnecting with our inner wisdom. As we learn more about ourselves, we start to shine and feel more confident. Here are a few more things to be aware of in the Superwoman camp that may cramp your style and make the joy of courtship elude you.

beware of princesses brandishing checklists!

This is yet another way old Superwoman attempts to control what is an unpredictable phenomenon – love! How about this for a conversation with a recent coaching client when I asked her about her dating strategy:

'Well, I am looking for a tall, handsome man, with his own teeth and hair, well groomed, well educated and wealthy. He will probably be a professional man like a stockbroker or lawyer. He must be in his forties, wise, with no baggage, no kids and preferably no ex-wives in tow. He will be ready to have children with me and I will become a full time, yummy mummy with a full time nanny, so I can spend my time at the spa, the gym and with my girlies on lunches, shopping and the odd charity function. My husband will come home from work at a reasonable hour so he can spend quality time with the children before dedicating the rest of his evening to me. We will holiday at least 3 times a year, live in a large country house and have all the typical trappings of a well-adjusted and affluent family.'

Whoa! Really, yes seriously, this was her real list. At this point my response was to leave the room in search of my magic wand!

Unfortunately, this is not the only time I have sat in awe as a single Superwoman has defined her wish list to me. Must have, must be, will not accept, must earn this, look like that, love this, hate that and so on. I am all for standards and having some clarity on what areas you will not compromise on in relation to your values, but beware the ever-growing set of demands. These will without question keep you single, and perfection is a dangerous game to play. If you expect all this from him, what will he expect in return? And can you live up to that? Bear in mind only princes and future kings marry princesses, and then only in fairy tales!

Love is so unpredictable, it hits you a moving train when you least expect it and from the strangest and most unlikely of places, but with a list like this you will probably not even recognise it! Learn to let go and surrender to the natural order of life – go with the flow. Checklists are for disobedient toddlers not sassy, sexy women in the zone! Being open to the possibility of love is not a project, a task or an item on your to-do list.

With so much judgement going on, so much control, so many demands, you are disregarding some amazing men that are right in front of you every day!

the sex in the city syndrome

Have you noticed how the dating scene has changed in the past 20 years? It used to be that men loitered around clubs and bars in packs and you could almost guarantee that any dance floor would be surrounded by guys looking on, surveying the talent and contemplating making a move. Oh how the scene has changed! Generally the dating behaviour of both sexes has merged and now you are just as likely to see women picking up men and drinking pints with their posse. This is one area where I am not convinced equality is doing us any favours. Before you launch into a rant, let me explain…

do you come here often love?

Regardless of who makes the first move in any come-on situation, women, generally, have always been in control. This goes back to the debate on energy and power. Women exert power by attraction. If they are grounded in their female energy they do not need to make any direct approach to a man, if they are interested in him, believe me, he will know! How? By signals, body language, eye contact, a smile, a slight move of the head, flick of the hair, a gentle touch or a smile as she glides past him on the way to the bar. This is about understanding how to 'work it' and although some women seem to have forgotten this skill, for many the power of attraction is alive and well. These women understand that sex appeal comes from self-confidence and self-love. A sexy woman walks with certainty, she knows who she is and makes no excuses or apologies. She has a sparkle in her eye, a bounce in her step and this is an irresistible attraction strategy. Know any? Superwoman thinks that behaving in this totally natural way is somehow selling out, or manipulation, or (heaven forbid) somehow cheap. Yet we are comfortable behaving like men and wonder why most of our conquests crash and burn. Whilst some guys may, initially, be flattered by an attractive women making the first move it will soon wear off if she attempts to keep control of the pace of courtship and continues to compete with him for his energy. Before you respond defensively by telling me the dating scene online is different – the dance floor may now be virtual, but the behaviour remains the same.

i can see you three weeks on tuesday...

Single Superwoman has such a busy life. Her schedule is maxed out with work, home and play so when a brave soul does finally pluck up the courage to take the long walk across the dance floor to make his move her response is generally, 'Well, my next available Saturday night is six weeks away!' Not the answer he was expecting and now, deflated, he walks away and you are left perplexed. You see, all those Saturday night booking are genuine fixtures for you, you were not giving him the brush-off, you were being honest so you are annoyed that he does not get that, right?

In conversation with Karen, a Superwoman single, the other day I enquired about how it was going with a guy she had recently had a first date with, a guy she had been crazy about for months. Here was her response:

'Well, I think he is another one that just loves the chase as he seems to have gone cold after we spent the weekend together. It is so depressing 'cos we had such a fab time together, we share the same sense of humour, we talked, we laughed, we got on so well and when it came to Sunday night and he enquired about seeing me again, naturally I got out my Blackberry and said my next available weekend was week ending 20th November. Well his face dropped and he simply said he could not make that and he would call me. That was 9 days ago and I am gutted but maybe he could not accept I am an independent, busy girl and he is just looking for some airhead bimbo. Oh well, his loss.'

But is it? You see week ending 20th November was 5 weeks away! What message was that giving him? Karen protested saying all her weekends were booked with genuine functions – Jo's first baby's christening; a spa weekend with the girls from work; a charity ball with the girls for which she'd spent weeks getting the right outfit; a shopping trip to Dublin with her sister; she'd agreed to go along to John's work's Christmas dinner so he was not on his own with a table full of couples; it was her best friend's anniversary of her divorce so they were going to party all weekend to keep her mind off it, etc. Do you see the challenge? You are so busy with your single life that he gets the distinct vibes that you have no time for him now or in the future and may decide that rather than get hurt or risk rejection he will just give it up as a bad idea. I know you may not be able to extract yourself from some of these commitments but being aware of this situation will encourage you to approach it in a more supportive way. So for example: 'I had a great time too and I really want to see you again soon but I know I have overbooked myself over the next couple of months; can we meet mid-week and I will see what shifts I can make to my weekend diary as it is a tad manic and **now** definitely needs some adjustments.'

He needs to feel important and have a tiny glimmer of hope that you would prefer to spend time with him, given a choice.

my girlfriends are my life, so deal with it...

How many times have you heard, 'Well, I don't need a man, it would be nice to have one and I miss a bit of male company and the physical side every now and again, but my friends keep me sane and my life is full.'?

Women that openly confess to not needing a man are unlikely to ever get one! Men need to be needed just like we do and the worst thing you can say to them (other than 'We need to talk') is 'I don't need you!'

This is old Superwoman stepping up again, scared of losing control, of being seen as weak, feeling unhinged at the thought of displaying an ounce of vulnerability.

But here's the thing: if all your emotional collateral is invested in your girlfriends, you confide in them about EVERYTHING, turn to them and only them in times of despair and joy, spend all your time thinking and planning activities with them, tell them your hopes, dreams, fears and stories and they take priority in your life no matter what – what is left for anyone else, in particular a man? In effect, what do you need a man for? Your emotional needs are sorted so the only thing you lack is the physical relationship, so guess what? That is exactly the level of relationship you will attract: a man who is simply looking for, or happy with, a physical relationship only. How can it be any other way? You have nothing else to give in return.

Does this make sense? I accept that girlfriends are important, I am not proposing you dump them when you bag a man, that is bad news too. I am simply recommending you get some balance and prioritise your time accordingly. A potential life partner deserves more of your life than your posse. Controversial?

Superwomen that have been single for a notable amount of time tend to align themselves with other professional singletons and this also keeps everyone single, for longer, as getting a man is seen as a betrayal and all the stops are pulled out to sabotage the woman who dares to appear happy and excited at having a man in her life. This is done on a subconscious level and driven by fear. Fear that they will be left on the shelf, be alone, have no support network, have no single friends, be isolated at functions, etc.

don't return to the scene of the crime

But for some of you, girlfriends are the tip of the iceberg: friendships with ex-boyfriends are far more problematic and in 99% of cases will keep you single – there, I've said it and wait, no, nothing – no lightning, no puff of smoke, still here.

There is no bigger turn-off or worry for a boyfriend than to be in a permanent competition with your ex or exes. I know you may not see it like this but for him is it primal. He feels constantly pitted against your past and quite often you have a lot of emotional baggage invested in these previous relationships that keeps you stuck. How tough is it for your current partner to be real with you, express his views and fears openly and connect if he is insecure about your past, a past that is still well and truly alive in your present? Your ex-partners know you very well, they know your buttons, your weaknesses, your vulnerabilities, so there is a tendency to stay connected to them emotionally and exclude your current partner in the process. The past is only useful to you if you wish to live there. Otherwise, move on girlfriend!

I know there is someone reading this now, tutting at me, saying 'Well, one of my ex-boyfriends was best man at my wedding and my husband and he are great pals.' I know, I know, life is full of exceptions so congratulations to you, but be aware, gifting your emotional self to the wrong man may cause dissonance in the strongest of relationships.

letting go of single superwoman....

Remember, a Diva is a woman who knows who she is and loves herself. She knows what is important to her and what she wants. She embraces her female energy, lives with balance, love, passion and authenticity and is a role model to

other women and young girls. She knows her greatness and shines.

Create space in your heart and your Blackberry for a man. De-clutter your life, it is not necessary to be active every night of the week. Be brave and spend some time with yourself in order to reconnect with your inner Diva!

'Working with Jane I have finally recognised that I can be successful, driven, vocal AND feminine and vulnerable. Before I never believed all of this could co-exist in the same person. For the past five years I have listened to all the classic quotes, 'Your knight in shining armour is just around the corner,' and 'Stop looking and he will appear,' but now several rather large pennies have dropped about my attraction strategy or lack of it! I now understand my behaviour around men better and they are no longer such a mystery to me, as I have obviously been to them!'

Rachel, Diva and travel entrepreneur

superwoman steps up as super boss 6

As more and more women successfully climb the corporate ladder, Superwoman becomes a formidable boss and learns to switch her male energy on full whack and go head to head with her male colleagues, or so she thinks.

climbing the corporate ladder – no place for a woman in her female energy, yet?

Now before I get lynched, let me be clear: I have absolute respect and admiration for women who make it in a man's world and if they make it without having to sacrifice their female energy then I have double respect for them, but guess what? I find it very hard to name more than a handful I have ever met that have managed this feat. In the testosterone-fuelled, male-driven corporate structures and cultures of today, holding onto your femininity demands courage, gumption and some visible signs that this is welcome in your workplace, more than tokenism at board level: female-friendly work practices, family leave as opposed to maternity leave, zero tolerance towards sexism and sexual harassment, and so on. We are a long way from finding these companies around every corner and I discuss this subject in more detail in my book **Diva Wisdom – Find Your Voice; Rock Your World And Pass It On** due for release in early 2015. We are new at this game, and it is a game. We have only been prominent in the workplace for the past 50-60 years and we are a long way from parity so I see women wearing their Superwoman cape as a shield and I understand why. To display vulnerability, to put your female energy up front and centre, to suggest there could be a different way to lead or manage, to talk as opposed to fight, to nurture as opposed to tell and so on could be seen as radical and 'not welcome here'!

when in rome...

We need to shift from ambition to inspiration, sales to service and competition to collaboration, all of which are easier to achieve with women on board. However, at the moment as women hit the top levels of middle management, their choices for survival and ascendancy are limited. They tend to have 3 choices:

1. Go native i.e. behave like a man, become one of the boys, don't rock the boat.

2. Continue to climb and become a trailblazer. This demands focus, a thick skin and finely tuned influencing skills with the acceptance that you will need to switch identities several times a day. It is emotionally exhausting and tough to sustain long term.

3. Get out.

Superwoman performs well in choice 1 but it is a tough place to live. Men don't particularly like women who behave like men, they may respect their toughness, but they never really accept them nor allow them access to the real party and they certainly don't respect them as girlfriends, equals, or colleagues. In fact, the stories of harassment, bullying and endemic sexism at this level would make your toes curl. This is a high price to pay for workplace recognition and I am in awe of women who can sustain this but I feel angry that this is still necessary and somehow a vicious circle, because if we do sustain this then men will see no reason to change or adapt their behaviour when women are in the room – arrrgh!

If we harnessed the power of sisterhood and refused to play this game, we could let Superwoman go and demand access to senior management on our own terms as women, grounded in our feminine energy, our natural place. Until then women will continue to take option 3 – get out – and over the past 10 years the mass exodus of women at senior management levels has hit 40%.[11] Yes, 40% of women are leaving and still nothing changes?

Whilst I continue to salute and champion the women out there making a difference, the trailblazers and the natives, if we are going to fix the talent leak anytime soon we need to stop fixing the women and start fixing the organisations.

Call it like it is – unconscious bias is endemic sexism, meritocracy means jobs for the boys and diversity means you can get to the top so long as you do not rock the boat, behave like a man and don't expect more than tokenism at best.

We need legislation but that is a different debate so let's stick to Superwoman for now!

how to keep superwoman in check at work
Well clearly if you are working in an organisation where female values are not welcome or recognised, Super-woman is a great shield and protector; but be aware at the end of the day the badge and cape must come

---

[11] Report by PricewaterhouseCooper (PwC), March 2007

off if you are going to have any quality of life at home with your husband/partner and/or your kids for all the reasons we discussed in previous chapters. This awareness is power but demands a bit more multi-thinking and processing as you need to switch identities between work and home. It is doable in the short term but can lead to challenges in the long term as the lines become blurred and Superwoman becomes dominant. She is a tough bird and the more validation she gets at work the harder she becomes to silence at home. You have been warned!

My career change was quite subtle from employee to management and due to this subtleness I didn't realise for many years that I was striving for perfection in most of my roles, wife, mother, daughter, boss, business partner, and client manager. However, life catches up with you and I think as time goes by, and dare I say you get a little older, you cannot keep up with the pace. It isn't necessarily about the hours you spend rather than the pace of life. All aspects are important and you try to be superhuman trying to juggle all and forget about you as an individual. Guilt is a major player that women seem to hold and this is sometimes the driving force – if I spend time at work, I need to then work extra hard at home and vice versa. The snowball starts and then you need someone to point out what's going on. This often needs to be someone away from your immediate pressure otherwise you are not likely to take any notice. If you invest in you and talk to someone else about this (I worked with Jane as my coach), in due course you start to realise what you are doing and although it's a scary feeling, you then find out that the way you have handled things is not always best for you and those around you. Awareness is power.

> *Jackie, Company Director, wife and mother of two children, one with Asperger's Syndrome*

Superwoman is alive and well in the world of entrepreneurship, in fact she is rocking her world as the leader of her own empire, generally an empire of one! This is because her control-freak tendencies and perfectionist mentality do not allow her to grow a business, they keep her firmly stuck in self-employment. Now before you all fight back, I know self-employment is a great option for many women and definitely a place many arrive at having left the untenable world of corporate. It offers more flexible working hours, less travel, and the ability to define your own style and approach. It is a smart choice and one that works well whilst children are young and your priorities need to be elsewhere. But if you want to grow a business, create some leverage, get some financial security and a kick-ass income you have to move beyond self-employment to growing a business with some legacy, and Superwoman is not friend of growth. Here's why...

Superwoman demands perfection and this stifles our business growth

We need more qualifications, a better website, more Twitter followers, more research and a knockout brand before we even dip our toe in the water. I cannot tell you how many times I have had this conversation: 'I am just not ready to take the next step yet. My website needs some work.' Ok, I say, so when? The reply, 'Well, we are on the 5th version now so hopefully this year.' Arrrrgh!!! It will never be perfect, perfect does not exist. My mantra is **GET GOING and GET BETTER**. The market cannot respond to what you are planning or talking about, it can only respond to what you put out there. To learn to swim you must first get in the pool! Just JUMP!

Superwoman is too emotionally attached to let go

A close ally of perfectionism is control. We believe no one can do all the work as well as us so we struggle to let go of ANYTHING!! We talk about not being able to find the staff, how it is easier to just do it ourselves, but this is exhausting and hampers any growth. This is all about our emotional attachment to our business. I hear women refer to their business as their 'baby' all the time and with this goes a reluctance and in some instances a real fear of letting go or allowing anyone else to look after their baby. We need to reframe this if we are to take our rightful place in the world of business. This control is all part of the Superwoman cape we wear with pride that needs to go and is discussed in the next section. We will not grow businesses without some external investment, a management team, Board of Non Execs etc. We could easily apply the baby analogy but in a different way: babies grow into children, teenagers then adults and along the way we as parents need to step back and let them make some of the decisions to build resilience and gain an element of independence. Bingo! Think about your 'business baby' like this and we could be onto a winner!

Super Boss got me working 24/7 with my team doing 9-5 and me feeling mentally and physically exhausted and my team feeling disempowered as I frequently redid their work – not good...

*Colleen, single mum with two teenage daughters,
running a design agency with 25 staff*

Superwoman is financially fearful
One of the key fears most women hold onto is the fear of debt, and because they associate growing a business with getting into debt they stay small and attempt to grow incrementally via their cash flow.

Now in exceptional circumstances this can work, but in most cases growth demands some form of financial investment and many women interpret this as debt and therefore undesirable. I am fascinated by this association as we do not do it with other capital investments. If I asked a group of women to raise their hand if they own their own home, most of the room would be ablaze with proud, outstretched arms but the next question, 'How many of you have a mortgage on this property?', shows me a very different picture. You see, you do not own your home if it is mortgaged. Stop your mortgage payments for 6 months and you will find out who owns your house! Yet we are comfortable with this debt, are we not? So could we not reframe financial debt to be an investment in our next 25-year future? Just a thought!

Financial institutions feed this insecurity by being far more cautious lending to women, hence why we are seeing a growth in female-led investment funds and business angels. I can fill a chapter on the stories women have told me about the inappropriate questions bank managers have asked them when they have asked for a loan or the impossible criteria requested for an overdraft and no, this is not the result of a tough economy when the same questions are not asked of men! Several times over my entrepreneurial career I have found it easier to secure a million pound investment than get a £5k overdraft.

Superwoman does not think she has the right skill-set

Are you kidding? Business today is about connection, making a difference and creativity – not got any of that then? We are natural connectors and relationship builders, our emotions can be used to our advantage as the majority of purchases are made by women, and show me a working mum and I will show you a formidable negotiator, top organiser and budgetary control genius! Business is no longer a ruthless standoff or an all-out battle to kill the competition, these are out-dated male models that worked when there was no other option, and I am thankful they did, but today there is a new energy, a more female-centric energy focussed on collaboration, values, team harmony, customer inclusion and flexibility. It is our time, ladies: we are on!

Superwoman has an unreasonable fear of failure

I say unreasonable because a fear of failure is a solid motivator for success, yet I see the most amazing, gifted and bright women staying small and insignificant for fear of failure and it breaks my heart. Failure is not personal, it is just the market telling you to move on, the world has changed, etc. Markets and customers change all the time. What was in last week is old hat tomorrow, and as entrepreneurs we need to keep abreast of this all the time. If we stop looking we will get caught out and this is when failure shows up. Quite often it is out of our control: a new competitor arrives, new technology changes the market overnight, etc. What I know for sure is that I have learned all my lessons on my knees in sight of failure. It is how I have built personal resilience, honed my passion and raised my game. I, like millions of entrepreneurs, am as proud of my failures as any of my successes and if you really want to walk the exciting and unpredictable path of entrepreneurship you have to embrace failure as a key element of the journey.

time to hang up the cape and rip off the invincible badge

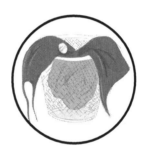

It is time, ladies – Superwoman has to go. Other than as a protective shield in the male-dominated world of corporate she is redundant and not supporting our cause in any way.

She is denying us our authenticity, she is keeping us from our greatness, she is stopping us from shining and she is NOT, and I repeat NOT, an empowering role model to pass on to our daughters.

I know it takes courage to let her go, to surrender to uncertainty and to embrace the occasional vulnerable moment but if we do not do this now, when will we?

the new rules

- Dump Little Miss Perfect, embrace the real you. Authenticity is real power, know who you are, know what you are capable of, know who your raving fans are, know your hot buttons, your passion and your needs, and compromise them at your peril.
- Know that striving for perfection at work and home is fake and weak. The business plan is never done, the website can always be improved, the kitchen could always be cleaner. Make your new mantra 'Get going and get better!'
- Embrace failure. We are supposed to make mistakes, it is the only way to build emotional resilience and it teaches us about life. If you are not making mistakes you are not risking enough or living your best life.
- Accept and give help. This is the new sisterhood. We are not supposed to be completely self-sufficient, we need community.
- Be proud to be an emotional creature, it is not a crime, it is real. Stop apologising and get over it!
- Value your uniqueness and teach your daughter to do the same – we are not all supposed to look or behave in the same way.

- Be kinder to yourself. Stop beating yourself up about your life choices and know that your best is good enough.
- And the big one: embrace your vulnerability. Have the courage and compassion to share your story, flaws and all. If you numb vulnerability you also numb joy.

Life begins at the end of your comfort zone

We have confused control with power

The Strong Woman Syndrome© appears to be a position of strength but in reality it is a place of weakness. Controlling everything does not give you power, it gives you a blinding migraine! It is emotionally exhausting to think that the only way to demand respect, or to be loved, or to be needed is to DO everything, for everyone, perfectly, all the time.

Real power comes from our authenticity. Real people make mistakes, real people learn and grow, real people embrace their vulnerability, or what Brene Brown calls their shame. Our shame is the fear of disconnection, if people find out about my weaknesses I will be alone. We are not supposed to be perfect. Superwoman is not strong she is, in fact, weakness personified and must go!

throwing away the cape and the invincible badge...

There is a better place to live. A more nourishing place, where you are allowed to embrace your vulnerability. A place where you can be true to yourself and be loved for who you are, not what you do or what you look like. A place where being female is a joy, where you can tap into your intuition, passion, emotions and courage. A place where it is OK to ask for help, to say no and to hand over control, sometimes!

I hope you give yourself permission to find this place some time soon. I have lived there for many years and although Superwoman may peek at me around the corner on days when I am over-tired and overwhelmed, I recognise her immediately, change my state, take a deep breath and allow myself to be imperfect!

Remember, a Diva is a woman who knows who she is and loves herself. She knows what is important to her and what she wants. She embraces her female energy, lives with balance, love, passion and authenticity and is a role model to other women and young girls. She knows her greatness and shines.

resources & references

This book is the result of my learnings and experience in working with thousands of women over the years, but I have also read extensively on this subject and I hereby pay tribute to all of the experts below whose work has been a great help to me in developing my opinions and conclusions.

Brown, Brene *The Gifts of Imperfection* (Brene Brown, 2010)

Doyle, Laura *The Surrendered Wife* (Simon & Schuster, 2001)

Doyle, Laura *The Surrendered Single* (Simon & Schuster, 2002)

Ensler, Eve *The Good Body* (Heinemann, 2004)

Ensler, Eve *I Am An Emotional Creature: The Secret Life of Girls Around The World* (Villard Press, 2011)

Heath, Susie *The Essence of Womanhood – Re-awakening the Authentic Feminine* (Ecademy Press, 2008)

Jeffers, Susan *Opening Our Hearts to Men* (Piatkus, 1990)

Oriah Mountain Dreamer *The Invitation* (HarperCollins, 1999)

Pease, Barbara & Allan *Why Men Don't Have A Clue & Women Always Need More Shoes* (Orion, 2002)

Williamson, Marianne *A Return to Love* (HarperCollins, 1992)

People to follow on Twitter

@Oprah

@CaitlinMoran – Times columnist, author of How To Be A Woman

@the3rdimagazine – global women in business magazine

@TEDxWomen – a global community of smart women

@GdnWomenLeaders – Guardian community to get more women to the top

@marwilliamson – author, spiritual teacher

@Shequotes – kick-ass quotes by amazing women

@Epic_women – celebrating some of the most amazing women ever to walk the planet

about the author

Jane Kenyon is 50 and excited to be starting the next act of what has been, so far, an amazing life. She is a serial entrepreneur, motivational coach, inspirational speaker, youth advocate, keen blogger and writer, ambassador for female empowerment and all round sassy Diva!

For the past 10 years she has worked exclusively with women and teenage girls via two aspirational brands she has created: **www.wellheeleddivas.com** and the social enterprise **www.girlsoutloud.org.uk**. Her passion for potential is contagious and despite many critical moments her courage to live life at the edge of her comfort zone is an inspiration.

You can engage with her today via the following channels:

On Twitter
@divadomrocks

On Facebook
https://www.facebook.com/jane.kenyon.50

On LinkedIn
http://uk.linkedin.com/pub/jane-kenyon

On Google+
https://www.google.com/+JaneKenyon1

On her blog
http://janekenyon.wordpress.com/

Find out how to become a Well Heeled Diva at **www.wellheeleddivas.com** and find out how to step up and become a role model Big Sister mentor to a teenage girl in the UK at **www.girlsoutloud.org.uk.**

Jane's second book *Diva Wisdom – Find Your Voice; Rock Your World and Pass It On!* will be out in early 2015. Sign up for her newsletter at **www.wellheeleddivas. com** to stay abreast of the publication date and her speaker engagements.

She lives in Cheshire, UK with her soul mate, the WW1 social historian Tony Davies, and her niece Holly.

Made in the USA
Charleston, SC
14 December 2014